MW00654696

THE PLACE OF WRITING

Hill of Howth, Summer 1982

THE PLACE OF WRITING

by
SEAMUS HEANEY

INTRODUCTION
by
RONALD SCHUCHARD

SCHOLARS PRESS
Atlanta, Georgia

EMORY STUDIES IN HUMANITIES

THE PLACE OF WRITING
by
Seamus Heaney

THE INAUGURATION OF THE RICHARD ELLMANN LECTURES IN MODERN LITERATURE

Library of Congress Cataloging in Publication Data

Heaney, Seamus.
The place of writing.
(Emory studies in humanities ; no. 1)
"The inauguration of the Richard Ellmann lectures in modern literature"--P. iii.
1. English poetry--Irish authors--History and criticism. 2. English poetry--20th century--History and criticism. 3. Ireland--Intellectual life--20th century. 4. Poetry of places--History and criticism. 5. Ellmann Richard, 1918- I. Title. II. Title: Richard Ellmann lectures in modern literature. III. Series.
PR8771.H4 1989 821'.009'89162 88-35568
ISBN 1-55540-315-8

Published by Scholars Press
for
Emory University
ISBN 1-55540-315-8

For Mary Ellmann

CONTENTS

Introduction

With *The Place of Writing* Seamus Heaney inaugurated the Richard Ellmann Lectures in Modern Literature at Emory University. The endowed Lectures honor the literary achievement of Richard Ellmann, who for a decade served the Emory community immeasurably as teacher, colleague and friend, becoming the University's first Robert W. Woodruff Professor in 1982. Prior to his association with Emory, Ellmann attained international prominence as a scholar and critic at Northwestern, Yale and Oxford universities, and for over forty years his writing set the highest standards of critical inquiry and humanistic scholarship. The biographer of James Joyce and Oscar Wilde, he enjoyed eminent domain among the interpreters of W. B. Yeats, Henri Michaux, Wallace Stevens and other modern writers. A soft-spoken teacher who was a taskmaster of substance and style, he inspired excellence in scores of students who are now leading scholars and critics in universities throughout the world. But the special legacy that Emory seeks to honor and perpetuate is the spirit of his public lectures, which were unparalleled in their appeal to a wide audience of readers, for he always spoke in a language that invited the general reader to share his personal engagement with serious literature.

Notified out of the blue that Ellmann would be in Atlanta the next day, Emory moved quickly to invite him to lecture for the first time in 1976. Word spread rapidly by mouth and radio, and by evening an unexpectedly large crowd had gathered to hear him speak on "A Late Victorian Love Affair"—a study of Oscar Wilde's destructive relationship with Lord Alfred Douglas, and the earliest preview of his magnificent biography of Oscar Wilde. A physicist who provided administrative support for the last minute lecture came up afterwards to say, sincerely, "That was the best lecture I ever heard." And that was all it took to pave the way for Ellmann's return as Visiting Professor the following year. Every spring for the next decade, when the Ellmanns, Dick and Mary, arrived in Atlanta with the blooming of the dogwoods, he brought with him a new public lecture—"The Uses of Decadence," "Oscar Wilde at Oxford," "Henry James Among the Aesthetes," "Freud and Literary Biography," "James Joyce: Side and Front Views," "W.B. Yeats's Second Puberty," "Samuel Beckett: Nayman of Noland"—a collective testament of his extraordinary range as a critic of modern letters.

The audiences that assembled for those lectures were unlike other university audiences. People from every academic department were there. Citizens of literature came from all over the Atlanta area to be there. They came not only because they had read his Yeats and Joyce in school, or because he was the foremost scholar of modern literature, or because the lectures were based upon the most rigorous research, or because he wore his learning so lightly—they came because they knew he addressed the common reader, because he illuminated the relation of literature and life, because he spoke with urbanity, with wry humor and wit, with an elegance and sureness of language not to be heard elsewhere. The presence of his *Oscar Wilde,* a major work of scholarship, on the *New York Times* best seller list underscores his natural relation with the general reader.

When it became evident that Professor Ellmann's illness would prevent his annual return in 1987, the University acted at once to endow in his name an annual series of lectures worthy in scope of his contribution to modern letters. President James T. Laney traveled personally to Oxford to tell him that the Lectures had been established. Then came the ineffable smile; he was immensely pleased. Asked whom he would like to inaugurate them, he replied softly, unhesitatingly, "Seamus." Three months later, on 13 May 1987, Richard Ellmann died.

The week of 11-15 April 1988 was thus the celebration of a great literary life, thanks to the generosity of people who came from across America and England to honor a friend, and to friends of the University who hosted spirited receptions and dinners. Seamus and Marie Heaney flew in from Harvard University, where he is Boylston Professor of Rhetoric and Oratory. Ellmann's son, Steve, flew in from the Columbia University School of Law to represent his family and to speak appreciatively to the audience on the endowment of the Lectures. Future lecturers are to be chosen by a rotating, international Selection Committee comprised of Ellmann's former friends, colleagues and students, and so the week received added buoyancy from the presence of Professors Barbara Hardy of Birkbeck College, University of London; Jon Stallworthy of Wolfson College, Oxford University; and Daniel Albright, of Rochester University. The Robert W. Woodruff Library mounted a special exhibition entitled "Eminent Domain: Ellmann Among Yeats, Joyce, Wilde and Heaney." Seán Ó Mórdha of Radio Telefis Eireann graciously provided the University with a copy of the RTE video production of Ellmann and Heaney in conversation, "Yeats, Joyce and Wilde." At mid-week the Selection Committee gathered for a discussion of Ellmann's life and work, and the videotapes of the discussion, the lectures and the readings are now in the University archives. Heaney gave a special reading for undergraduates of the poetry of Louis MacNeice and contemporary poets of Northern Ireland discussed in the lectures, and the poet was to give a most moving reading of his own poems to conclude the week. His poem in memory of Ellmann, "The Sounds of Rain," published in a special edition for the occasion, provided the title for the reading, which was attended by an enthusiastic audience of over a thousand people from the Atlanta area. In such ceremony the achievement of a great scholar and friend was duly honored, the legacy of his lectures perpetuated.

II

Seamus Heaney's *The Place of Writing* originates in his longtime preoccupation with the unstable role of place in the creative process. The aura of place imposes itself on one poet's imagination; another poet imposes his singular vision on a plural place; places become havens or heavens; they drive the poet into spiritual or physical exile; they provide poetry with its nourishment and its distraction; they liberate imagination and darken consciousness. Heaney's disinterested investigation of place focused initially on Northern Ireland but soon expanded to include an international community of poets at their separate frontiers of writing. His continuous consideration of the poet in his historical place generates a dialogue between the aims of art and the claims of history, between an emerging artistic consciousness and a persistent historical conscience. The essays on place that precede *The Place of*

Writing are practical, to the extent that they aim to illuminate the context and enlarge the audience of recent poetry in Northern Ireland, and personal, to the extent that they attempt to work out in the public arena of critical discourse, from the perspectives of literary history and the political present, the tensions that his native Ulster engenders in his own writing. In his Richard Ellmann Lectures, Heaney returns to the real and symbolic places of Irish writers in three lectures that at once expand and intensify the uneasy relation of place, poetry and politics in modern literature.

The pleasures and problems of place spark from the poetic workshop in "The Sense of Place" (1978), where, against the legendary backdrop of Yeats's Celtic Twilight and the vivid localities of Dante's *Commedia,* Heaney explores the ways in which his admired seniors, Patrick Kavanagh and John Montague, poetically engage their respective geographical places in creating a "country of the mind." Where Kavanagh faithfully attaches himself to the countryside and dialect of Co. Monaghan in a celebration of the parochial and the present, Montague religiously detaches himself from the countryside of Co. Tyrone, perceiving places as mythic, tribal palimpsests inscribed with his rich psychic heritage. If the point of view that issues from Kavanagh's poetry is as apolitical as it is communal, Heaney only hints at "an element of cultural and political resistance" in Montague's poetry, where the places are more central to the poetry than an impinging political reality. Heaney also downplays the political tensions at work in the poetry of yet a third senior poet, John Hewitt, whose poetic instincts are also deeply rooted in Irish places but whose intelligence is founded on the reality of the British realm, on Unionist traditions and allegiances. While recognizing Hewitt's bifocal point of view, Heaney upholds the poetry itself as a separate, distinctive realm, asserting that "it is in the rag-and-bone shop of the instincts that a poetry begins and ends, though it can raise itself by the ladders of intelligence towards a platform and a politics." Only in concluding the essay does he intimate that for the poets of his own generation, namely Derek Mahon, Paul Muldoon and Michael Longley, the operation of place in the creative process has radically altered. Place has come to symbolize not a communal situation but a personal conflict between an ideal Ulster of the mind and a predatory Ulster of the present, a drama that deeply affects the action of their art:

"None of these poets surrenders himself to the mythology of his place but instead each subdues the place to become an element in his own private mythology. They may be preyed upon in life by the consequences of living on this island now, but their art is a mode of play to outface the predatory circumstances."

Heaney did not have occasion to elaborate the "mode of play" affected by the "predatory circumstances" of these three poets until 1984, when he spoke at Wordsworth's Dove Cottage on "Place and Displacement: Recent Poetry of Northern Ireland," delivered shortly after the publication of *Sweeney Astray.* Appropriately, he characterizes their contemporary predicament through the analogy of a disaffected Wordsworth suffering among patriotic neighbors and worshippers in England during the French Revolution:

> The good place where Wordsworth's nurture happened and to which his habitual feelings are most naturally attuned has become, for the revolutionary poet, the wrong place. Life, where he is situated, is not as he wants it to be. He is displaced from his own affections by a vision of the good that is located elsewhere. His political, utopian aspirations deracinate him from the beloved actuality of his surroundings so that his instinctive being and his appetitive intelligence are knocked out of alignment. He feels like a traitor among those he knows and loves. To be true to one part of himself, he must betray another part. The inner state of man is thus shaken and the shock waves in the consciousness reflect the upheavals in the surrounding world.

In the face of such an intolerable reality, the poet's artistic drive—or psychological compulsion in Jungian terms—is to move to a higher level of consciousness and resolve the conflict symbolically in art. Heaney, motivated in part to explain the preoccupation with poetic form and the alleged reticent response to violence among poets in Northern Ireland, draws upon the Jungian model to assert just such a relation between poetic technique and historical situation. The contemporary poet in Ireland is compelled to "outstrip" the unbearable political reality of Ulster, to transcend it in highly formal lyrics, to enter the linguistic "mode of play" that momentarily intensifies him and detaches him from his predatory circumstances. To Heaney, the poetic transcendence is not an evasion of sympathy with national conditions but rather a transposition of that sympathy into symbol. In his own reading of the poems of

Mahon, Muldoon and Longley, he points to the symbolic and allegorical substrata running beneath the formal surfaces, fully aware, however, that "the reading of those political implications is in itself a political activity, separate from the processes that produced the poems, an extension or projection from the artistic endeavour which is not obliged to have any intention beyond its own proper completion." The displaced poet's symbolic resolution of his conflicts in lyric form remains an artistic, self-healing process, and in the poems of his contemporaries Heaney finds the process "neither deliberately provocative nor culpably detached."

Heaney dramatizes a similar conflict and process in *Sweeney Astray*, his translation of the ancient *Buile Suibhne*. Mad Sweeney, a Celtic king changed into a bird and exiled to the trees by a Christian saint, symbolically resolves his purgatorial plight in poems that name the flora and fauna of places that nourish his imagination. As Heaney consciously instructs the reader, "insofar as Sweeney is also a figure of the artist, displaced, guilty, assuaging himself by his utterance, it is possible to read the work as an aspect of the quarrel between free creative imagination and the constraints of religious, political, and domestic obligation."

So persistent had this quarrel become in Heaney's imagination that he sought extended critical company among those writers outside of Northern Ireland for whom the issues of debate were redoubled in intensity. He identified with poets from the Eastern bloc, particularly the Russian writer Osip Mandelstam and the Polish writers Zbigniew Herbert, Czslaw Milosz and Anna Swirr, but also with a number of international poets who know the reality of the governed tongue, the constrained imagination, the accused conscience. In "Place, Pastness, Poems" (1985) he reached out to include Pablo Neruda, the Chilean poet who "is tormented by the injustice of history and his past is accusatory," and, perhaps surprisingly, the American poet John Crowe Ransom:

> Like Auden, Ransom was at a detached angle to what he cherished. He was in two, maybe three places at once: in the parochial south, within the imposed Union, and inside the literary 'mind of Europe.' He was in place and displaced and consequently his poetic challenges and their resolutions were tactical, venturesome and provisional. His plight was symptomatic of the double focus which the poet from a regional culture is now likely to

> experience, caught between a need to affirm the centrality of the local experience to his own being and a recognition that this experience is likely to be peripheral to the usual life of his age.

In this world-wide company of "displaced" poets, all of whom proclaim the autocracy of art, Heaney was moved to lead the poetic reconstitution of what he calls "The Republic of Conscience," where all representatives are charged "to speak on their behalf in [their] own tongue," knowing that no ambassador "would ever be relieved."

The inevitable leader of the Republic is Dante, appointed by Heaney for his masterful accommodation of the political and the transcendent. In "Envies and Identifications: Dante and the Modern Poet" (1985), Heaney explores the ways in which poets from different countries have responded to Dante's influence, particularly Osip Mandelstam, who, straining against the pressures placed on his poetry by the Stalinist regime, found in Dante an "inner freedom" for his shackled imagination. To Mandelstam, says Heaney, Dante becomes "the apotheosis of free, natural, biological process, as a hive of bees, a process of crystallization, a hurry of pigeon flights, a focus for all the impulsive, instinctive, non-utilitarian elements in the creative life." The great irony in Mandelstam's creative life is that the very act of writing was an act of conscience, an imaginative obedience to the necessity of art. Though Heaney's countryman, Thomas Kinsella, receives only passing mention in this Dantean context, Heaney urges a study of Kinsella's "exploration of the individual's quest for coherence and integrity in a world of constant disintegration and slippage." Heaney initiates that study here in his third lecture, "Cornucopia and Empty Shell."

Heaney's envy of and identification with Osip Mandelstam was followed by a re-vision of poets and poetic processes. "I have learned to value this poetry of inner freedom very highly," he writes in his reconsideration of Patrick Kavanagh's poetry, "The Placeless Heaven" (1987). Nine years earlier he had described Kavanagh's early poetry as being grounded in the physical reality of Co. Monaghan, much as his own early poetry was grounded in Co. Derry. When Heaney discovered Kavanagh in the 1960s he was caught up by the possibilities for his own poetry of "the unregarded data of the usual life" and experienced "a primitive delight in finding world becoming word." He had long overlooked the transformation from an outer to an inner reality that takes place in Kavanagh's later poetry, where places have become "luminous spaces within his mind. They have been evacuated of their status as background, as documentary geography, and exist instead as transfigured images, sites where the mind projects its own force." Kavanagh records the meditative and visionary turn in "Auditors In":

> From the sour soil of a town where all roots canker
> I turn away to where the Self reposes
> The placeless Heaven that's under all our noses
> Where we're shut off from the barren anger

The "Self," says Heaney, was for Kavanagh, as for Mandelstam, a "redemptive force that maintained the artist's inner freedom in the face of worldly disappointments, an infrangible dignity." The redirection of the poetic mind from external place to spaces in the Self is also evident in "In Memory of My Mother," where Kavanagh fills her historical absence with her visionary presence. The method of the poem seems to inform Heaney's "Clearances," an elegiac sonnet sequence in memory of his own mother. In the final sonnet the visionary poem fills the vacant space of a felled chestnut tree planted at his birth:

> I thought of walking round and round a space
> Utterly empty, utterly a source
> Where the decked chestnut tree had lost its place
> . . .
> Its heft and hush become a bright nowhere,
> A soul ramifying and forever
> Silent, beyond silence listened for.

Ironically, as Heaney moves toward a greater visionary freedom in *The Haw Lantern* (1987), in another quarter of the mind the weight of history tightens its rein on the poet's conscience.

Heaney's discovery of Kavanagh was coincident with his discovery of Louis MacNeice. He heard MacNeice read his poetry, bought and admired his *Collected Poems*, but the younger poet could not close the distance between them. "His poems arose from a mind-stuff and existed in a cultural setting which were at one remove from me and what I came from. . . . I envied them but I was not taken over by them the way I was taken over by Kavanagh." This passing account of his initial response to MacNeice was, like the previous mention of Kinsella, a mental marker, for MacNeice commands Heaney's reconsideration here in the second lecture, "The Pre-Natal Mountain."

The presence who presides with Dante over the foregoing essays, as the themes and authors come forward to *The Place of Writing*, is Yeats, whose writing life in Thoor Ballylee is the subject of the opening lecture. Heaney first broached the question of Yeats's legacy to Irish writers in "Yeats as an Example?" (1978). Even then, what he found most admirable in Yeats, who felt strongly the poet's difficult "choice" between the life and the work, "is the way his life and his work are *not* separate but make a continuum, the way the courage of his vision did not confine itself to rhetorics but issued in actions." Observer of Yeats in action as a young poet and later as an established poet and public figure, Heaney was in awe of the energy and integrity with which Yeats pursued his ideal vision of art and culture, wondrous of how Yeats could be at once an artist and a magician, "a Celt, with a lifeline to the mythological depths," and "a propagandist, with a firm line for journalists." In one of his last, Dantean poems, "Cuchulain Comforted," Yeats seems to Heaney to bring all of his powers as maker and thinker together in a poem of "rich and strange conclusiveness," an ideal melding of life and art. "It is a poem deeply at one with the weak and the strong of this earth, full of a motherly kindness towards life, but also unflinching in its belief in the propriety and beauty of life transcended into art, song, words." But at the essay's end Heaney's Yeats looms as a larger-than-life figure, a shrouded Cuchulain of immense authority, a poet whose exemplary powers remain an ideal to contemplate, not a reality to emulate.

And yet the example was to abide. Four years later, Radio Telefis Eireann filmed "Joyce, Yeats and Wilde" (1982), showing Richard Ellmann and Seamus Heaney in Dublin as they walked and talked about the authors and the places they inhabited. Ellmann, intrigued by Heaney's remarks on poetry and politics, asked him to clarify again what was exemplary in Yeats. "Well," Heaney replied,

> in terms of the writer conducting himself in a politicized milieu, I think Yeats become important within that milieu not so much for what he says as for who he is. Within a culture the most important thing for the poet is to establish authority, and Yeats had the gift of establishing authority: first of all by achievement, but secondly by a conduct which was 'majestic' in some kind of way and overbearing to some extent but based upon a belief in the culture. He could rebuke the culture because he was its most intense representative to some extent. And I think that the poet has to not get caught in a position where he is answerable to the politician but where in some way the politician is under his spiritual gaze. Now that is what is exemplary about Yeats, but also what is very difficult to achieve for a writer in contemporary Ireland.

From the beginning of his career, Yeats indeed refused to let poetry become a handmaiden to politics, and while he relentlessly upheld the reality and integrity of the poetic process he willfully stepped out of his writing to speak on public platforms and in newspaper columns against the eviction of tenants by English landlords, royal visits to Ireland, atrocities in the colonies, censorship of art, confiscation of Hugh Lane's pictures, and so on until the outspoken poet became a Senator of the Irish Free State. Thus *The King's Threshold* (1904) was to Yeats no mere dramatization of a Celtic tale; it was more the drama of his personal determination to return the poet's voice to the center of Irish culture. While Joyce and Stephen Dedalus headed into exile, Yeats and Seanchan "pleaded for the poet's right,/Established at the establishment of the world," to sit with the Bishops, Soldiers and Makers of the Law,

> Who long had thought it against their dignity
> For a mere man of words to sit amongst them
> At the great council of the State and share
> In their authority.

While Yeats knew, as Auden finally discovered, that "poetry makes nothing happen," he believed that the poet himself should not be passive, that he should be passionately true in public to his private images of justice, reality and wisdom.

As Heaney traced the predicaments of place in writers from Northern Ireland and the Eastern bloc, his own drama with English editors and the media began to mount, a drama that developed inevitably from his being an Irish poet widely praised, published and honored in England. The turning point came when an anthology in which he was a featured poet was, to his utter dismay and displacement, generically titled *The Penguin Book of Contemporary British Poetry*. The crisis followed: "For weeks and months," he wrote publicly to his editors in "An Open Letter" (1983), "I've messed about,/Unclear, embarrassed and in doubt,/Footered, havered, spraughled . . . /Wondering should I write it out /Or let it go." Driven out of silence by an insistent muse, he diplomatically but uncompromisingly reminded his editors in epistolary sestets that "My passport's green," that he had never toasted a sovereign who "from the start [of] her reign/Of crown and rose/Defied, displaced, would not combine /What I'd espouse." Home ground had to be stood:

> You'll understand I draw the line
> At being robbed of what is mine,
> My *patria*, my deep design
> To be at home
> In my own place and dwell within
> Its proper name—
>
> Traumatic Ireland! Checkpoints, cairns,
> Slated roofs, stone ditches, ferns,
> Dublin squares where sunset burns
> The Georgian brick—
> The whole imagined country mourns
> Its lost, erotic
>
> *Aisling* life.

The letter signed, the quandary of the poet's conduct in history began to press upon the poetry. Richard Ellmann, in his review of *Station Island* (1984), was shrewd to see in specific poems how the situation in Ulster now pervaded the poet's imagination: "He hunts for precedents for his own feelings, and lights on Milosz's sense of being caught between participating actively in history and contemplating a motionless point, and on Chekhov's recognition of slavery on Sakhalin even as he tries to waken the free man in himself" (*NYRB*, 14-3-85). More dramatically, in the title poem the poet's pilgrimage to Lough Derg leads to visionary encounters with shades who, like his murdered cousin, lay on the guilt for the poet's inaction, for having "confused evasion and artistic tact":

> 'The Protestant who shot me through the head
> I accuse directly, but indirectly, you
> who now atone perhaps on this bed
> for the way you whitewashed ugliness and drew
> the lovely blinds of the *Purgatorio*
> and saccharined my death with morning dew.'

The only solace from chastisement comes from the shadowy exile, James Joyce, who would have the poet turn from the mournful claims of political agonies to the self-haven of his art. "And don't be so earnest," Joyce admonished, "let others wear the sackcloth and the ashes":

> That subject people stuff is a cod's game,
> infantile, like your peasant pilgrimage.
>
> You lose more of yourself than you redeem
> doing the decent thing. Keep at a tangent.

Concluded Ellmann sympathetically, but on the Joycean side: "In a no-win situation, the poet's duty is to register compassion, not partisanship."

In "The Government of the Tongue" (1987) Heaney does indeed reaffirm his conviction "that poetry is its own reality and no matter how much a poet may concede to the corrective pressures of social, moral, political and historical reality, the ultimate fidelity must be to the demands and promise of the artistic event." Nevertheless, as Joyce well knew, the poetic imagination cannot repress its *agenbite of inwit*, and in *The Haw Lantern* that remorse of conscience is often a catalytic agent in the creative act. It is felt in the intense scrutiny of "the roaming shape of Diogenes/with his lantern, seeking one just man"; in the command that the verdict for "a lifetime's speechlessness" be like "the judgment of Hermes,/ God of the stone heap, where the stones were verdicts/Cast solidly at his feet"; in the painful trope of "a man on a springboard/Who keeps limbering up because the man cannot dive"; in the eschewal of the "guardian angel of passivity" in the poet's expectant search for

> one among us who never swerved
> from all his instincts told him was right action,
> who stood his ground in the indicative,
> whose boat will lift when the cloudburst happens.

In the process of writing his Ellmann Lectures at Harvard last spring, just as a new round of horror grew from the deaths of Provisional IRA and British soldiers in Belfast, Heaney was placed in the difficult position of being called to London to receive the *Sunday Times* award for excellence in writing. On 28 March, having seen British press accounts and television coverage of the separate burial rites and suffering, Heaney stepped out of his place of writing, and out of the "polite meaningless words" of the evening to rebuke the British government and media for breaking the spirit of a recent Anglo-Irish agreement. Designed to create an atmosphere for communication, the agreement called upon both parties to hold to a mutual respect for political fact, to strive for a mutual recognition of political fiction, and to avoid posturing on the moral high ground in time of conflict and outrage:

> I noticed in yesterday's newspapers an inclination to view the British army presence in Ulster once again as part of the solution rather than part of the problem, an inclination to view them as hygienic, rubber-gloved, impersonally-motivated technicians operating in polluted ghettoes where indigenous hatreds are cultured in self-induced and self-wounding conditions. I noticed an inclination to think of military funerals as a tribal and undesirable form of solidarity when enacted on the Falls Road, but as somehow immunised against tribal significance when the victims were British soldiers, the mourners were British parents, and the martial music was relayed with deeply emotive effect by the news channels of British television. The so-called 'spirit of the agreement' is not against the solemnisation in public of national sorrows, but it is surely against the gradual obliteration from public British awareness of a realisation that policies which Downing Street presumably regards as a hard line against terrorism can feel like a high-handed disregard for the self-respect of the Irish people in general; and it should be against any downplaying of the fact that local Belfast paranoia--generated by a recent

> graveyard bombing and shooting--played some part in the shamefully automatic cruelty and horror of the two British soldiers' deaths which followed.

"It would perhaps be adept to avoid facing this issue," he told his audience, but with the shade of Robert Lowell at his side he asserted in Lowell's words that "'every serious artist knows that he cannot enjoy public celebration without making subtle public commitments.'" And then he summoned the shade of Yeats:

> Yeats's challenge to the writer was to hold in a single thought reality and justice, and the same challenge is in effect in Westminster and Fleet Street. . . . My plea, therefore, is for a renewed self-consciousness in the expression of just national concerns by the British media, an avoidance of the high ground, and an ongoing example of the free, self-regulating debate which has typically distinguished the British democratic process.

In making the plea, he read in a "spirit of exasperation" the words of King Cormac to the young, wisdom-seeking Carbery in eighth-century Ireland:

> Be not too hard nor too feeble . . .
> If you be too hard, you will be broken.
> If you be too feeble, you will be crushed.
> ("Anglo-Irish Occasions," LRB, 5-5-88)

In this hard-won, liberated moment of forthright speech, with the banquet under his gaze—in this public moment of artistic recognition, with the writing honored for its excellence and integrity—Seamus Heaney instinctively assumed his authority as Irish poet--not consciously as a spokesman for Ulster, and not in the grand manner, but as a dual citizen of the Commonwealth of Art and the Republic of Conscience. An Irish poet had crossed the sovereign's threshold; his voice had been heard in the sovereign court of media: Yeats would have loved every minute of it.

Within a fortnight Heaney arrived at Emory University to inaugurate the Richard Ellmann Lectures in memory of his friend. In the lectures published here, which he delivered then with gathered force of mind and voice, Heaney continues to probe the creative tensions and political challenges in the writing of his countrymen: Yeats, MacNeice and Kavanagh, Mahon, Muldoon and Longley, Montague and Kinsella, Beckett and Friel—all are present. What unfolds in his addresses on place in the creative process is the *sensibility* that informs modern Irish writing, such as readers have not witnessed since Ellmann made accessible the sensibilities of Yeats, Joyce and Wilde. In that these lectures are part of an ongoing exploration of the relation of significant life and significant art, they are a fitting tribute to Richard Ellmann's legacy to modern letters: he would have loved every minute of them.

Ronald Schuchard
Atlanta, Georgia

Author's Note

When Professor Ronald Schuchard telephoned me from Oxford early in 1987, to invite me to Emory University the following spring, Richard Ellmann was still living at his Oxford home in St. Giles, loved and cared for by his family and devoted friends. I was sensible of the high regard implicit in the invitation but daunted also by its high demands, since the Richard Ellmann Lectures in Modern Literature would be measured against the unique standards of excellence that he represented. Nevertheless, the fact that Dick had assented to my being asked, and the knowledge that I had the approval of a selection committee both distinguished and friendly, emboldened me to accept.

During the second week of April this year, when the lectures were delivered, my initial sense of privilege was richly extended. Everyone who assembled for the occasion seemed to do so with a specific personal commitment; one had a feeling that the immense, equable force of Ellmann's personality, scholarship and teaching was being celebrated in a deliberate and truly ceremonial way. At the formal hospitalities surrounding the inauguration of the series, at the informal but no less hospitable gatherings that ended each day, and on the occasions of the lectures themselves, there was a constantly renewed awareness that we had come together because we cherished a man of irreplaceable worth. Underlying the rightly public aspect of the events, there was an unusual prevailing mood of tenderness and loss.

Throughout the week, many people contributed to the thoroughness of the welcome that surrounded my wife, myself and all the other guests of the University. We all felt the benefit that accrued from President Laney's personal support of the proceedings, and from Tom Bertrand's attentive executive care; and Randy Brandes's assiduity as chauffeur and guide kept us happily on time and on course. Daniel Albright, Barbara Hardy, Jon and Jill Stallworthy, Richard and Susan Murdoch all found themselves enjoying hospitality that grew more and more spontaneous for having been so well and truly prepared. None of our hosts, however, will count themselves less thanked if I mention here in particular the names of Ron and Keith Schuchard. Their friendship had been the bonus of previous visits to Emory; during this one, their characteristic merriment, steadfastness and perfect intellectual pitch added the final seal of rightness to a gathering which Richard Ellmann would have recognized and approved as "A scene well set and excellent company."

Seamus Heaney
Dublin, July, 1988

The Place of Writing: W.B. Yeats and Thoor Ballylee

One of the happiest moments of my life was a sunlit September morning in 1982 when Richard Ellmann and I walked all around the Hill of Howth above Dublin Bay, chatting about the way that place had figured in the imaginations of James Joyce and W. B. Yeats. The fact that we were being filmed for a television documentary did not lessen the pleasure. Indeed there was a sense in which it increased it, since the programme was in fact a homage to Ellmann. In that year of the centenary of Joyce's birth, Ireland, through the agency of its national television station and the good offices of RTE producer Seán Ó Mórdha, was formally saluting the epoch-making achievements of this great biographer and critic. In the 1950s and 1960s Richard Ellmann's books had established the image and confirmed the authority of the major twentieth-century Irish novelist and of the major twentieth-century Irish poet as well. Yet those onlookers who materialized once the cameras began to roll would never have guessed from Dick's unpretentious manner that here was one of the country's unofficial national treasures.

It is therefore a great honour for me to have been invited to initiate the treasuring process which this lecture series will represent at Emory University. Ellmann was a scholar and biographer of unparalleled scope and meticulousness, one who possessed a commanding sense of the whole outline of his subjects and a delicate capacity for eliciting fully-fledged meaning by brooding upon details. He was also a critic with a unique double gift: his illuminations were as felicitous as his judgments were authoritative. He could maintain subtle, receptive vigilance over a text and explicate it within the idiom of his profession; but he could also produce a kind of Johnsonian meditation that considered what the text was worth to the fuller enjoyment or better enduring of our unspecialized lives.

This was because his writing, like his conduct, came out of that place from which, according to the poet Ted Hughes, the truest poetry also comes: the place in us where our ultimate capacity for suffering and decision is lodged. To meet Richard Ellmann was to encounter a gathered force. I was always moved by a feeling that innate gifts of fortitude, tenderness and fairness had been consecrated to a discipline, one which placed immense intellectual and personal demands upon him but which rewarded him with a rock-bottom emotional verity. In Keats's terms, he was an intelligence who had been schooled into a soul, and the good consequences for all who knew him are palpable here this evening.

But to go back to Howth Head, on that September morning in 1982. Our director, Seán O Mórdha, was a film maker of rare sensitivity and intelligence, one with whom Dick collaborated happily and rewardingly in the last decade of his life; he was also an editor and critic with an intense commitment to literature in the Irish language. The vitality of the indigenous tradition remains a matter of living concern for him. It was natural, therefore, that he wanted me, as the official interlocutor, to lead our guest towards some statement about the way Irishness became operative or better still definitive in the works of Yeats, Joyce and Wilde, the three Dubliners whose achievement we were to explore in a "commodious vicus of recirculation" over the next couple of days. Had Ellmann not reminded us that Yeats, as a child living in Howth, used to seclude himself in a clump of rhododendrons? And had he not gone on to make this a significant detail in the biography of the poet whose imagination would always be sympathetic to solitary withdrawn figures like Parnell? So could the biographer not be encouraged to make a few bold generalizations about the link between origins and genius? In what way was Ireland part of the specifically artistic action of these epoch-making writers? What was the relationship between writing and place?

That Richard Ellmann managed to elude any simple answer to these questions should be sufficient warning of their difficulty, even perhaps of their fatuousness. We are more and more aware of writing as a place in itself, a destination in art arrived at by way of art. And yet an urge persists to enquire into the inspiration and foundation which place affords in the creative process. When I think, for example, of Archimedes's famous claim that he could move the world if he could find the right place to position his lever, I sense that it has a deep applicability to this question of the writer and his enabling ground. Is there not something here analogous to what happened when J.M. Synge located himself and his subjects on the Aran Islands? The lever of his imagination then began to work: in a metaphoric extension of the scientific definition of work, we can say that it then managed to move a certain force through a certain distance. His force became efficacious. On Aran, he was at last properly positioned and enormously capable as a result.

Synge's home address was suburban Dublin but his imaginative home was in the solitude of Wicklow or West Kerry or Aran: the obviousness of this truth does not diminish its mystery. So in these three lectures I want to take up the theme again, in loving memory of our Dublin perambulations, in further homage to Dick's great spirit and great work, and with gratitude and pride at having been given the honour to stand here, in the place of speaking, at Emory University. Tonight's lecture approaches the topic by way of Yeats's tower at Ballylee in Co. Galway. The process by which this postal address becomes a poetic symbol is the very subject of many of Yeats's poems in the 1920s, so we shall be on familiar ground and I shall be intent on making two simple, important points: that the poetic imagination in its strongest manifestation imposes its vision upon a place rather than accepts a vision from it; and that this visionary imposition is never exempt from the imagination's antithetical ability to subvert its own creation. In other words, once the place has been brought into written existence, it is inevitable that it be unwritten. This perception will then be fundamental to my second lecture, in which I take on the vexed question of poetry and politics in contemporary Ireland, in order to examine how different political and cultural dispositions get expressed in poetry at a level below the professed meanings and espousals of the poems themselves. The third lecture will come at related concerns, considering the work of some Irish poets and playwrights in the light of an image which Richard Ellmann took from Yeats, and which I have pirated and further elaborated.

The usual assumption, when we speak of writers and place, is that the writer stands in some directly expressive or interpretative relationship to the milieu. He or she becomes a voice of the spirit of the region. The writing is infused with the atmosphere, physical and emotional, of a certain landscape or seascape, and while the writer's immediate purpose may not have any direct bearing upon the regional or national background, the background is sensed as a distinctive element in the work.

This filial relationship with region did indeed work for the young Yeats and the Sligo countryside should arguably be called the Young Yeats Country. But in this lecture I am concerned with the poet from the age of fifty onward, establishing an outpost of poetic reality in the shape of a physical landmark, a poet with a domineering rather than a grateful relation to place, one whose poems have created a country of the mind rather than the other way round, (and the more usual way) where the country has created the mind which in turn creates the poems.

Consider, for example, Thomas Hardy's home in Dorset, in the hamlet of Upper Bockhampton. Set among the trees, deep at the center of a web of paths and bye-roads, in the matured stillness of an old garden, small-windowed, dark-ceilinged, stone-floored, hip-thatched, the Hardy birthplace embodies the feel of a way of life native to the place. It suggests a common heritage, an adherence to the hearth world of Wessex. If it is a secret, it is not singular. We recognize a consonance between the inside and outside of that house and the center and circumference of Hardy's vision. Hardy country, in other words, predated Hardy. It awaited its expression. Its ballad memory, its Romano-Celtic twilights and nineteenth-century dawns, all of which are part of the phantasmagoria of Hardy's work, were already immanent there as that from which Hardy sprang. He did not impose Hardiness upon his landscape the way Yeats imposed Yeatsiness upon his. He was patient rather than peremptory, bearing the given life rather than overbearing it. Hardy's eye was as watchful and withdrawn as the little window at the back of his birthplace through which his mason father doled out wages to the workmen. But it was nevertheless an eye which functioned within its community as unremarkably as the hatch functioned in the wall.

Or take Max Gate, the house Hardy designed and had built for himself on the outskirts of Dorchester, the house that proclaimed him the distinguished writer rather than the son of a Bockhampton builder: here the emblematic meaning is greatly different from the meaning of the tower which Yeats restored for himself and his wife at a corresponding moment of his career. Even if we recognize a significance in its alignment with the birthplace across the fields,

Max Gate does not seek the status of the monument. It is a red-brick dwelling place, which belongs to the fashion of its period and maintains the decorum of its suburb. It both embraces and embodies ordinariness, if only as a camouflage or a retreat; it certainly does not proclaim itself or its inhabitant as an original, a founder, a keeper, a sentry or a besieged one.

Yeats admittedly spent most of his life in houses which were equally machines for living in. The house where he was born in Sandymount Avenue in Dublin remains the usual semi-detached, mid-Victorian, bay-windowed, steps and basement type of residence which would be hard to mythologize beyond its solid bourgeois respectability. The same is true of his apartments in Bloomsbury and the town house in Dublin's Merrion Square which was his main base during the very time when the later tower poems were being written. These addresses were not significant and would not be made to signify in terms of Yeats's imagining. They remained structures which would never become symbols. They were places where Yeats would remain his unwritten self.

But a Norman keep in the Barony of Kiltartan, dating from the thirteenth or fourteenth century, descending from the great line of the de Burgos, and registered in *The Booke of Connaught* at the end of the sixteenth century, this was a very different matter. Even though Yeats bought it for £35 from a government body called with an unromantic grimness The Congested Districts Board, it retained for him the aura of its historically resonant past and became a verifying force within his mind. It sponsored an attitude and a style, attained in his books a fabulous second dimension that would eventually transform its original status as a picturesque antiquity in the fields of Ballylee.

Mary Hanley and Liam Miller, whose pamphlet on the tower and its history I am gratefully drawing upon here (*Thoor Ballylee*, Dolmen, 1965), have documented Yeats's negotiations thoroughly and shown that it is not just within the poetry that the tower's force and effect are registered. From the moment he began to make plans for its restoration, there is a sense of occasion in Yeats's letters. We recognize that a ceremonious action is being undertaken. His negotiations with builders and architects are heightened and solemnized by the tone, as though he were a Renaissance Pope or a Tuscan duke commissioning masters. A boozy professor of architecture becomes a genius. The adjective "great" begins to intone itself like a mantra. Here he is, writing to John Quinn on July 23, 1918:

> We are surrounded with plans. This morning designs arrived from the drunken man of genius, Scott, for two beds. The war is improving the work for, being unable to import anything, we have bought the whole contents of an old mill—great beams and three-inch planks, and old paving stones; and the local carpenter and mason and blacksmith are at work for us. On a great stone beside the front door will be inscribed these lines:
>
> I, the poet, William Yeats,
> With common sedge and broken slates
> And smithy work from the Gort forge,
> Restored this tower for my wife George;
> And on my heirs I lay a curse
> If they should alter for the worse,
> From fashion or an empty mind,
> What Raftery built and Scott designed.

Nothing Hardyesque about that. And all the while, William Scott was designing what his employer designated "great" chairs and tables, and "great" elmwood beds, and ceilings which would be painted with magical stars and angles, as befitted a castle. For a castle it was and a castle Yeats inclined to call it, as in the following letter to his father on July 16, 1919. By now his wife and young family have been able to move in, but the passage conjures up not so much a family home as a Homeric chamber: the word "hall," for example, gradually attains the legendary amplitude or Hrothgar's Heorot or Thomas Moore's Tara:

> I am writing in the great ground floor of the castle—pleasantest room I have yet seen, a great wide window opening over the river and a round arched door leading to the thatched hall. . . . There is a stone floor and a stone-roofed entrance-hall with the door to winding stair to left, and then a larger thatched hall, beyond which is a cottage and kitchen. In the thatched hall imagine a great copper hanging lantern (which is, however, not there yet but will be I hope, next week). I am writing at a great trestle table which George keeps covered with wild flowers.

A month before, Yeats had completed the mighty rhetoric of the poem he called "A Prayer for my Daughter," so it is no surprise to discover a similarity of tone in the letter and in the last stanza of the poem. Both conceive of a house as a ritually disposed and ceremoniously bedecked enclosure, and the final lines of the poem explicitly link the possibility of ample, innocent life to the dream of a house self-consciously high-mannered and liturgical:

> And may her bridegroom bring her to a house
> Where all's accustomed, ceremonious;
> For arrogance and hatred are the wares
> Peddled in the thoroughfares.
> How but in custom and in ceremony
> Are innocence and beauty born?
> Ceremony's a name for the rich horn,
> And custom for the spreading laurel tree.

Wonderful melodies; and given the fact that Yeats himself was still a bridegroom of sorts when he wrote these lines—less than three years married—one could be forgiven for discerning in them as much a paean to the house he was preparing for his young wife as a prayer for his infant daughter.

Three years had passed between Yeats's purchase of the tower in 1916 and that summer of 1919 when he and George moved in; but even then, the residence was never to be permanent. Thoor Ballylee remained a kind of summer home, occupied occasionally by the family between 1919 and 1928, after which date their visits ceased altogether. By then, Yeats's health was beginning to fail. Moreover, in 1928 the volume of poems entitled *The Tower* appeared, and its sequel, *The Winding Stair* (1933), had been conceived. The tower had now entered so deeply into the prophetic strains of his voice that it could be invoked without being inhabited. He no longer needed to live in it since he had attained a state in which he lived *by* it.

To call it a summer home, then, is really slightly off the mark, since it is obvious that the tower's first function was not domestic. Here he was in the place of writing. It was one of his singing schools, one of the soul's monuments of its own magnificence. His other addresses were necessary shelters but Ballylee was a sacramental site, an outward sign of an inner grace. The grace here was poetry and the lonely tower was the poet's sign. Within it, he was within his own mind. The posture of the building corresponded to the posture he would attain. The stone in all its obstinacy and stillness, the plumb bulk and resistant profile of the keep, the dream form and the brute fact simultaneously impressed on mind and senses, all this transmission of sensation and symbolic aura made the actual building stones into touchstones for the work he would aspire to. And that work would have to be a holding action in the face of old age, death and the disintegrating civilization which he, "Heart smitten with emotion," perceived in its decline.

One of the first functions of a poem, after all, is to satisfy a need in the poet. The achievement of a sufficient form and the release of a self-given music have a justifying effect within his life. And if the horizons inside which that life is being lived are menacing, the need for the steadying gift of finished art becomes all the more urgent. So it is in the light of just such a constantly flickering horizon of violence and breakdown that we must read the tower poems and much else of Yeats's work at this period.

The Easter Rising had occurred in Dublin a few months before his negotiations with the Congested Districts Board in 1916. The Battle of the Somme was fought that summer also. The Russian Revolution broke in 1917. From 1919 onwards, the War of Independence was in full swing in Ireland, and between 1922 and 1923, the Civil War got close enough to Ballylee for the builder, Thomas Rafferty, to get shot, for the bridge outside the tower to get blown up, and for the mind of this most public-spirited of poets to be darkened by a sense of personal danger and civic collapse.

So it is no wonder that the plough was set deeper into the emotional ground than ever before. If refuge within a medieval keep had given Yeats intimations of a new authoritativeness, the authoritativeness could not be credible to him until the poems were there like ramparts thrown up to prove that he had survived the onslaught of menacing circumstance. Richard Ellmann, for example, long ago noted how insistently the first person possessive figures in the subtitles of "Meditations in Time of Civil War": "My House," "My Table," "My Descendants," "The Road at My Door," "The Stare's Nest by My Window." With characteristic insight, he found in all this a symptom of the fully empowered imagination, Yeats as a man of means and position living in a microcosm where, in Ellmann's persuasive formulation, "life is condensed and controlled by the mechanism of symbolism." Yet I would want to add a corollary and suggest that this obsessive "my" is also conceivably a symptom of a last ditch stand. The poet, thrown back within the final personal ring of defense, is forced into single combat with old age and with history and can employ as weapons only those things which lie most nakedly to his hand or most indelibly inside his mind.

For example, "My House," the second poem in the sequence, begins and accumulates its force as a pile-up of nouns wrested from the air and placed like builder's blocks in a course of stonework, each block handled and fitted without the benefit of mortar, which is to say that the nouns function without the bonding action of a main verb. There are thirteen lines of dense affirmative word-chunks which convey an opaque feeling of constituted strength, of gathered, battened-down, self-absorbed power. This is writing which has, to be sure, an immediate covenant with the substantial world, yet the words operate perhaps more as a phonetic element than as a referential system.

> An ancient bridge, and a more ancient tower,
> A farmhouse that is sheltered by its wall,
> An acre of stony ground,
> Where the symbolic rose can break in flower,
> Old ragged elms, old thorns innumerable,
> The sound of the rain or sound
> Of every wind that blows;
> The stilted water-hen
> Crossing stream again
> Scared by the splashing of a dozen cows;
> A winding stair, a chamber arched with stone,
> A grey stone fireplace with an open hearth,
> A candle and written page.

At this point the turn arrives: at the culmination of physical and linguistic density, enter a Platonist. Typically, Yeats's imagining could not repose for too long in the consolations of the material world. It is as if at the climax of solidarity, at the very apotheosis of body-strength and world-thickness, the language calls forth an antithetical mind-strength; as if the noun cores burst and erupt a magma of verb fire.

If this is to overdramatize the case, it is not misrepresent it. The visionary process that is sketched in "My House" when the wind changes its theme at line 14 is magnificently evoked in another tower poem, "Blood and the Moon:"

> The strength that gives our blood and state magnanimity
> of its own desire;
> Everything that is not God consumed with intellectual fire.

In that poem, after all, Yeats espouses Bishop Berkeley's conviction that if the mind changes its theme, then "this pragmatical, preposterous pig of a world, its farrow that so solid seem,/Must vanish." The world does not, of course, vanish in this section of "Meditations in Time of Civil War," nor is the apocalypse of "all things consumed in intellectual fire" attempted. Nevertheless, the poem does proceed to concentrate its focus inward so that the fortress of stone passing into the fortress of words becomes finally a manifestation of the fortified mind, besieged yet ablaze, exalted and incontrovertible:

> *Il Penseroso's* Platonist toiled on
> In some like chamber, shadowing forth
> How the daemonic rage
> Imagined everything.
> Benighted travellers
> From markets and from fairs
> Have seen his midnight candle glimmering.
>
> Two men have founded here. A man-at-arms
> Gathered a score of horse and spent his days
> In this tumultuous spot,
> Where through long wars and sudden night alarms
> His dwindling score and he seemed castaways
> Forgetting and forgot;
> And I, that after me
> My bodily heirs may find,
> To exalt a lonely mind,
> Befitting emblems of adversity.

This poem and the sequence of which it forms a part are ultimately about artistic faith, about trusting images and emblems rather than conventional readings of the world, about holding fast, living in a fastness, fastening the mind upon the certain tragedy of one's extinction and still refusing, even in the face of that extinction, to cede the value of what Yeats calls elsewhere "The spiritual intellect's great work."

There is a transcendent imperative in the image of the tower. It is true that in Yeats's mind it was also linked to the Anglo-Irish tradition, and symbolized the historical bonds of ancestry and inheritance, but its virtue effectively released his consciousness from the exorbitance of the historical. For example, at the historical moment of "Meditations," Yeats's espoused caste, the Protestant Ascendancy, were being given notice that their influence and control were at an end in a newly independent, mainly Catholic Ireland. Outside his poems, Yeats would identify with them in an understandably partisan and political way, most notably in his Senate speech of 1925 when he spoke against a bill which was to make divorce illegal in the new Free State. Again it was Richard Ellmann, writing in *Yeats: The Man and the Masks* (1948), who acutely suggested that Yeats spoke on that occasion in the service of class rather than of principle. The speech reveals the nexus of haughty if not snobbish social attitudes which underlie his more exposed and existential stance as heroic solitary in a candle-lit cell. The famous lines are these:

> I think it tragic that within three years of this country gaining its independence we should be discussing a measure which a minority of this nation considers to be grossly oppressive. I am proud to consider myself a typical man of that minority. We against whom you have done this thing are no petty people. We are one of the great stocks of Europe. We are the people of Burke; we are the people of Grattan; we are the people of Swift, the people of Emmet, the people of Parnell. We have created the most of the modern literature of this country. We have created the best of its political intelligence. Yet I do not altogether regret what has happened. I shall be able to find out, if not I, my children will be able to find out whether we have lost our stamina or not.

What in these stung lines is combative and vindictive in a class-conscious way becomes visionary and stoical in the third section of "Meditations," the poem called "My Descendants." In it, the future into which Yeats's children must live is envisaged as non-chivalric and anti-aristocratic, the very antithesis of all that the poet cherishes; yet the poem, unlike the speech, attains a spirit of equanimity. It can bear to contemplate the affront which reality will offer his expectations. Here is not simply nostalgia for the vanished glories of the Anglo-Irish, not a jeremiad upon the filthy modern tide, but a steady gaze at the consequences of his own perception that "man is in love and loves what vanishes."

> And what if my descendants lose the flower
> Through natural declension of the soul,
> Through too much business with the passing hour,
> Through too much play, or marriage with a fool?
> May this laborious stair and this stark tower
> Become a roofless ruin that the owl
> May build in the cracked masonry and cry
> Her desolation to the desolate sky.
>
> The Primum Mobile that fashioned us
> Has made the very owls in circles move;
> And I, that count myself most prosperous,
> Seeing that love and friendship are enough,
> For an old neighbour's friendship chose the house
> And decked and altered it for a girl's love,
> And know whatever flourish and decline
> These stones remain their monument and mine.

Here the place of writing is essentially the stanza form itself, that strong-arched room of eight iambic pentameters rhyming *abababcc* which serves as a redoubt for the resurgent spirit in poems like "Sailing to Byzantium," the first section of "Nineteen Hundred and Nineteen," "Among School Children," "Coole Park and Ballylee, 1931" and several of his other definitive works. In these poems, the unshakably affirmative music of this *ottava rima* stanza is the formal correlative of the poet's indomitable spirit. The complete coincidence between period and stanza which he had begun to strive for compounds utterance with architecture, recalls Milton's figure of the poet as one who builds the lofty rhyme and also recalls Yeats's own stated desire to make the tower a permanent symbol of his poetic work, "plainly visible to the passer-by."

In the case of the poem we have just read, the tower calls him from propaganda towards prophecy. It would have him exalt vision rather than salt the historical wound. The tower may be crumbling into a destructive future, but that very crumbling is part of an inexorable reality which the mind must accept as truth. Yet the mind, once it has digested this knowledge, is still not permitted to renege on its challenge, not allowed to cave in to a passive acceptance of the deplorable. Its responsibility to its own affirmative project is not absolved by its perception of the foredoomed nature of that project.

All of this remains implicit in the pitch and roundedness of the poetry in "My Descendants," but it is proclaimed confidently and explicitly in a poem composed in 1926, the year after the Senate speech. In the title poem of *The Tower* volume, Thoor Ballylee is not just picturesque nor simply emblematical of the menaced splendours of a particular cultural heritage. It is rather a podium from which the spirit's voice can best be projected. In the third section of this poem, the tower's stoniness is repeated in the lean, clean-chiselled obelisk of the verse-form; its head-clearing airiness is present in the rise and enjambement of the three-stressed line. Indeed, the tower is now not just an embodied attitude or symbol of loyalties but also a pure discharge of energy. Inevitably, it continues to affiliate Yeats with his caste and casts him as its self-appointed panegyrist. But it also marks an original space where utterance and being are synonymous. This section of "The Tower" so strives to transcend its personal and historical occasion that it reminds us of the exultation and absolutism of another tower-dwelling visionary, Rainer Maria Rilke. It was Rilke who declared in his third sonnet to Orpheus, written in 1922, only a few years before Yeats's poem, that *Gesang ist Dasein,* singing is being, or song is reality, phrases that could easily stand as epigraph to Yeats's superb peroration:

> Now shall I make my soul,
> Compelling it to study
> In a learned school
> Till the wreck of body,
> Slow decay of blood,
> Testy delirium
> Or dull decrepitude,
> Or what worse evil come—
> The death of friends, or death

Of every brilliant eye
That made a catch in the breath—
Seem but the clouds of the sky
When the horizon fades;
Or a bird's sleepy cry
Among the deepening shades.

One brilliant eye which had made a catch in the breath in nineteenth-century Ballylee was the beauty Mary Hynes, celebrated in song by the blind poet Anthony Raftery. Both of them are invoked in an earlier part of "The Tower," but all through this period of his writing, Yeats was in the situation dramatized in another famous Raftery poem:

Mise Raifteirí an file,
Lán dóchas 's grá,
Dul siar ar mo thuras
Le solus mo chroí.

Féach anois mé
Mo chúl le balla,
Ag seinm ceoil
Le póchaí folaimh.

I am Raftery the poet,
Full of hope and love,
Going westward on my journey
By the light of my heart.

Look at me now,
My back to a wall,
Playing music
To empty pockets.

When he quartered himself and his poetry in Thoor Ballylee, Yeats was similarly backed into an extreme position. He was being compelled by his years and his times into a new awareness of himself as his own solitary protagonist out on the mortal arena, and suddenly in that needy space, a tower ascended. Not a tree, as in Rilke's first sonnet to Orpheus, not a natural given miracle but a built-up, lived-with, deliberately adhered-to tower. Yet by now that tower is as deep inside our hearing as the temple which Rilke imagines the god Orpheus building inside the listening consciousness of the creatures. Before the visitation of his song, their ear was full of humble, un-self-trusting creaturely life, shabby huts full of common speech and unpoetic desultoriness. But his song brought about a marvel.

> A tree ascended there. Oh pure transcendence!
> Oh Orpheus sings! Oh tall tree in the ear!
> And all things hushed. Yet even in that silence
> a new beginning, beckoning, change appeared.
>
> Creatures of stillness crowded from the bright
> unbound forest, out of their lairs and nests:
> and it was not from any dullness, not
> from fear, that they were so quiet in themselves,
> but from simply listening. Bellow, roar, shriek
> seemed small inside their hearts. And where there had been
> just a makeshift hut to receive the music,
>
> a shelter nailed up out of their darkest longing,
> with an entryway that shuddered in the wind—
> you built a temple deep inside their hearing.

That sense of a temple inside the hearing, of an undeniable acoustic architecture, of a written vaulting, of the firmness and in-placeness and undislodgeableness of poetic form, that is one of Yeats's great gifts to our century; and his power to achieve it was due in no small measure to the "beckoning," the "new beginning," the "pure transcendence" of an old Norman castle in Ballylee, a place that was nowhere until it was a written place.

Yet we must go further, since Yeats himself went further. Another of his gifts was his own boldness to question the final value and trustworthiness of this powerfully composed tower in the ear--for it is a mark of the fully empowered imagination that it shirks none of the challenges that the fully awakened intelligence can offer it. The last stanza of "All Souls Night," for example, represents the positive force that Yeats's tower-schooled mind could command: his prayer for concentration is itself focused and shining with an inward, self-directed illumination:

> Such thought—such thought have I that hold it tight
> Till meditation master all its parts,
> Nothing can stay my glance
> Until that glance run in the world's despite
> To where the damned have howled away their hearts,
> And where the blessed dance;
> Such thought, that in it bound
> I need no other thing,
> Wound in mind's wandering
> As mummies in the mummy-cloth are wound.

I have talked mostly about this kind of centered, purposeful writing because it is what we rejoice at most immediately in Yeats's poems. Here conviction has arisen out of the very words in which it is sought, and stamina has been conjured by the strong expression of his own need for it. But, as Richard Ellmann has insisted, the credibility of this art is ultimately guaranteed by Yeats's readiness to doubt its efficaciousness. The very power of his desire for foundedness should alert us to the fear of unfoundedness which might lurk beneath it, what Philip Larkin called "the solving emptiness/That lies just under all we do." It is Yeats's greatest triumph that he could acknowledge this possibility and yet maintain a resolute faith in the worth of artistic creation. In a late poem like "Man and the Echo," the much-vaunted insulation of the tower dweller—that quarantined, stone-kept otherness of the artist—is helpless against the unaccommodated cry of suffering nature. The man's composure is certainly assailed by the mocking echo of his own doubting mind, but it is finally most vulnerable to the yelp of pain in a hurt creature:

> But hush, for I have lost the theme
> Its joy or night seem but a dream;
> Up there some hawk or owl has struck
> Dropping out of sky or rock,
> A stricken rabbit is crying out
> And its cry distracts my thought.

It is the triumph of this art to confront a despair at the very notion of art *as* triumph. Yet it also manages to wrest from the confrontation with such despair a margin of trust that makes the renewal of artistic effort contemplatable. Behind the large firm gestures of Yeats's last poems, where the humanist effort is racked upon a wheel that is a paradigm of hollowness, we can already make out the shuffling, unappeasable decrepitude of Beckett's heroes going on refusing to go on.

I will return to these concerns in the third lecture, since they constitute the theme from Ellmann that I wish to address. Here, in conclusion, I shall follow his lead to "The Black Tower," the last poem which Yeats composed. This poem dramatizes, with an almost scampish offhandedness, a dialectic between the spirit's indomitable, affirmative impulses and the mind's capacity to ironize and mock those impulses as self-serving fictions. The indomitable aspect is reflected in an ancient motif of warriors buried in a standing position, signifying their eternal vigilance and oath-bound fidelity to the cause that unified them during their lives. The ironist and questioner is their old cook, who represents a kind of unheroic life force, a scuttling principle of survival and self-preservation. He embodies all that Cuchulain had come to terms with in the poem "Cuchulain Comforted" when the hero goes to the underworld and must consort with "Convicted cowards . . . by kindred slain/'Or driven from home and left to die in fear.'" Yet the cook's thoroughly creditable scepticism is resisted by the *comitatus*; they persist at their post even as they are pestered by his rumours and heckling. They are like T. S. Eliot's magi journeying towards an ambiguous epiphany with voices singing in their ears that this may be all folly:

> Say that the men of the old black tower
> Though they may but feed as the goatherd feeds,
> Their money spent, their wine gone sour,
> Lack nothing that a soldier needs,
> That all are oath-bound men;
> Those banners come not in.
>
> *There in the tomb stand the dead upright,*
> *But winds come up from the shore;*
> *They shake when the winds roar*
> *Old bones upon the mountain shake.*

In this final appearance of Thoor Ballylee in Yeats's poetry, it stands fast and Yeats stands by it. Both tower and poet stand, as Macbeth and Macbeth's castle once stood, suspended in art time, ratified by a prophetic utterance. In Shakespeare's play, Macbeth's sense of inviolable sanctuary was based on oracles delivered to him when the witches prophesied that he would be safe until Birnam Wood should come to Dunsinane. Yeats, on the other hand, had written his own oracles to himself and created a fortified space within the rooms of many powerfully vaulted stanzas. But just as the witches equivocated and the world as a wood of trees moved unthinkably to dislodge Macbeth, so in the end the Yeatsian keep of tragic commitment and loyalty is assailed by mutinous doubts about the ultimate value of what there is to keep. Nevertheless, the Yeatsian drama ends with the poet as Macbeth, still pacing the battlements, just acknowledging the tremor on the fringes of Birnam but refusing to allow his chivalric countenance to quail. The tower as emblem of adversity, as the place of writing, has taken on a final aspect as icon of the absurd. And it is because of the way these manifold, extreme and unshirked recognitions are embodied in Yeats's poems that we know again that poetry is truly a vision of reality, and the creative imagination a truth-seeking and truth-augmenting faculty.

The Pre-Natal Mountain: Vision and Irony in Recent Irish Poetry

In the first lecture I touched on one implication of my general title, "The Place of Writing." By examining how the obduracy of Yeats's tower got translated into an enabling strain in his poetic voice, I hoped to show how topographical place could become written place; how the felicitous conceit of a stanza being a room got verified in poetry whose syntactic and metrical vaulting was the equivalent of that "chamber arched with stone" in which Yeats composed the syntax and metre of his own stanzas. To trace the process of this translation was to discover again one of the first principles of art work, a principle which (I suggested) might be enunciated in terms of the old schoolbook definition of the meaning of work in any context, artistic or otherwise. This used to be expressed as follows: to work is to move a certain mass through a certain distance. In the case of poetry, the distance moved through is that which separates the historically and topographically situated place from the written place, the mass moved is one aspect of the writer's historical/biographical experience, and each becomes a factor of the other in the achieved work. The work of art, in other words, involves raising the historical record to a different power.

Helen Vendler has recently described the nature of this power as symbolic, and in my second lecture I want to explore the question of the status we are to assign to such symbolic utterance within the historical circumstances where we live our lives. The question is not just academic. For the last twenty years, it has been more or less present in the minds of Irish poets, Polish poets, South African poets, West Indian poets (those in London as well as those in the Caribbean) and many others. All these have been caught at a crossroads where the essentially aesthetic demand of their vocation encountered the different demand that their work participate in a general debate which preoccupies their societies. The topic of this debate typically concerns the political rights and cultural loyalties of different social or racial groups resulting from separate heritages, affronts and identities; and even if individual poets have been spared direct pressure to address those concerns in their work, they would need to have been insensitive in a disqualifying way not to feel the prevalent expectation—if only as an anxiety about their creative purposes.

It is true that such anxiety can be allayed by recognizing the ultimate truth of Yeats's declaration that "art/Is but a vision of reality"—and therefore to be distinguished *qua* art from rhetoric or sentiment. Yet to proceed to the liberties which this password opens up without being aware of its cost, in terms of the moral and ethical imperatives subsumed in it, is to proceed too nimbly. Even such a student of the aesthetic as Roland Barthes immediately concedes the distress latent in the writer's apparent absolution by form. "Form," Barthes writes in the Introduction to *Writing Degree Zero*,

> hovers before his gaze like an object; whatever he does, it is a scandal: if it stands resplendent, it appears outmoded; if it is a law unto itself, it is asocial; in so far as it is particular in relation to time or mankind, it cannot but mean solitude.

This solitude of the poet has nevertheless been embraced by many as the condition proper to our times, and—if the place be Ireland—proper to our place. In Ireland, north and south, one of the effects of the renewed British/Irish troubles over the last couple of decades has been a tendency to view with grave suspicion any idiom that might possibly be construed as nationalistic. But in fact, the prevailing neglect of Yeats's admonishment of future generations of Irish writers to maintain their covenant with an oppressed past and "be/Still the indomitable Irishry" preceded the 1970s campaign of violence mounted in the name of Ireland by the Provisional IRA; already, in the 1950s, Patrick Kavanagh had coined the term "buck lepping" to discredit the element of extravagant gesture and picturesque speech which were the *sine qua non* of a stereotypical Irish bard. In an article as critically intelligent as it was personally merciless, Kavanagh had anatomized the synthetic Irishry of a man he dubbed "the gallivanting poet," Yeats's friend and protégé, F. R. Higgins. "Almost everything about Higgins," Kavanagh wrote, "needs to be put in inverted commas." Kavanagh also wrote elsewhere that such "Irishism" was a form of anti-art, a way of posing as a poet without really being one, and all through his *Collected Prose* (1967), keeps reiterating his conviction that the "so-called Irish Literary Movement . . . was a thoroughgoing, English-bred lie" because of the way it promoted the exotic and pastoral aspects of the country, bypassing its authentic Catholicism and enervation with a compensatory fantasy of pagan and heroic survivals.

After 1969, however, there was a more than literary motive for such castigation of the myth of Ireland as a spiritual entity, a mystical principle which could elicit the religiose devotion of not only the young Yeats but also of the executed poet and revolutionary, Padraic Pearse, martyr of Easter 1916 and sponsor of the blood-sacrific strain in Irish republicanism. With the outbreak of civic violence in Belfast and Derry, Irishism was perceived to be not only a manifestation of ethnic kitsch but potentially a code that spelled loyalty to the aims and (by extension) the methods of the IRA. Hence, as the seventies advanced, it became increasingly difficult to express fidelity to the ideals of the Irish Literary Revival, which were essentially born of a healthy desire to redress the impositions of cultural imperialism, without seeming to become allied with a terrorist campaign that justified itself by self-righteous rhetoric against British imperialism of the original, historically rejected and politically repugnant sort.

Add then to the first native literary backlash and to this subsequent political one a third factor deriving not only from a deconstructionist suspicion of the ideological depth-charges in all literature, but also from well-urged doubts about the very possibility of justified language arts after Auschwitz: it all added up to a situation in which the literary intelligentsia of Britain and Ireland were anxious to confine the operations of imaginative writing to a sanitized realm that might include the ludic, the ironic, the parodic, the satiric, the pathetic, the domestic, the elegiac and the self-inculpatory, but which would conscientiously exclude the visionary prophetic, the patriotic witness, the national epical. It was not the place of writing to encompass these ends any more. Because of their dangerous availability for co-option as generalized herd-emotion, and their bias towards inflation and slither, these latter modes are tacitly deemed to be obsolescent. The poet who would resuscitate them faces not just an understandable resistance in his audience, attuned with good reason to the new poetry's sceptical lightness of being; he faces also an ingrained reluctance within poetic language itself to enter ever again into its nineteenth-century collusion with the business of elevation, exhortation and expostulation.

Nowadays we typically think of art as a means to redress or affront public and historical conditions. The danger is that we might go so far in this direction as to confuse the salutary scandal of such confrontation with the craven scandal of evading or absconding from historical conditions altogether. In fact the dice are so loaded against the old form of engagement represented by the Rupert Brooke who wrote "If I should die, think only this of me,/ That there's some corner of a foreign field/That is forever England," and the prejudice against poetry as a self-conscious function of the national culture is so strong, that even to canvas the idea of connection between a founded nation and a founded poetic voice is in danger of being judged old-fashioned, if not downright retrograde. It is more than ever true that "Under bare Ben Bulben's head/In Drumcliff churchyard Yeats is laid"—for it would seem that the orders he issued from under the mountain have been effectively countermanded.

One of the most resourceful in changing the demands and pointing to a new agenda for Irish poetry is the young northern poet, Paul Muldoon, whose recent book, *Meeting the British* (1987), engages in a typically ventriloquistical dialogue with the genius of Drumcliff. The lines I quoted here sound forthright, but they are from a dramatic monologue attributed to W.H. Auden and occur in a daring poem entitled "7 Middagh Street." (This was the address of a house in Brooklyn inhabited for a while in the early 1940s by a cast of characters that included Auden himself, Chester Kallman, Gypsy Rose Lee, Carson McCullers, Erica Mann, Salvador Dali and Louis MacNeice). Yet even if the lines are voiced for Auden, a notable sceptic when it came to the question of art's relation to action and its value as an influence in public affairs, we will be justified in hearing in them an expression of a point of view by Muldoon:

> And were Yeats living at this hour
> it should be in some ruined tower

not malachited Ballylee
where he paid out to those below

one gilt-edged scroll from his pencil
as though he were part-Rapunzel

and partly Delphic oracle.
As for his crass, rhetorical

posturing, 'Did that play of mine
send out certain men (*certain* men?)

the English shot . . . ?'
the answer is 'Certainly not'.

If Yeats had saved his pencil-lead
would certain men have stayed in bed?

For history's a twisted root
with art its small, translucent fruit

and never the other way round.
The roots by which we were once bound

are severed here, in any case,
and we are all now dispossessed;

prince, poet, construction worker,
salesman, soda fountain jerker—

all equally isolated.
Each loads flour, sugar and salted

beef into a covered wagon
And strikes out for his Oregon,

each straining for the ghostly axe
of a huge, blond-haired lumberjack.

Auden's sexual quest, indeed his sexual zest, is here very nicely woven in with Muldoon's sense of the Whitmanesque liberation and democratic scope of America. By placing the action in the melting pot of New York and by making the speaker the defensive and decamping Auden, Muldoon manages to give edge and justification to those gibes against Yeats's grand rhetorical question. It is all of a piece with the introduction to Muldoon's recent anthology, *The Faber Book of Contemporary Irish Poetry* (1986), in which he seems to deride the notion that poetry might have a desirable, never mind a demonstrable, relation to the life of a nation. To get involved with such ideas, he implies, is at best to commit a literary offence, at worst to promote dubious mystiques involving race memory and the chosen people complex.

What Muldoon does is to print, without comment, an extract from a BBC radio broadcast made in 1939, in which Louis MacNeice (not yet in Middagh Street, but already very much a leading light among British poets of the 1930s) discusses poetry with F. R. Higgins. Higgins, old gallivanter that he was, not unexpectedly came on as the advocate of a kind of poetry destined to raise the eyebrows, if not the hackles, of the more cosmopolitan MacNeice.

The programme was broadcast by the Northern Ireland service of the BBC, in acknowledgement no doubt of MacNeice's own Northern Ireland connections. He had been born in Belfast in 1907, although he moved soon with his family to the Co. Antrim town of Carrickfergus where, as he wryly observes in the poem called "Carrickfergus," "I was the rector's son, born to the anglican order,/Banned for ever from the candles of the Irish poor." Later, in a long poem written before the autumn broadcast and called with a journalistic aptness "Autumn Journal," MacNeice had made a fierce reckoning of his relationship with Ireland, concluding that "She is both a bore and a bitch," who gives her children little to fit them out for a world where "common sense is the vogue." So there he was, back in the studios of Belfast, and when he faced F. R. Higgins at the microphone, he may well have remembered his rebuke to the country and been tempted to blare it across the table at his interlocuter. "I hate your grandiose airs,/Your sob-stuff, your laugh and your swagger,/Your assumption that everyone cares/ Who is the king of your castle." Here, at any rate, are a couple of the things which Higgins said across the table to MacNeice:

> *Higgins*: Present-day Irish poets are believers—heretical believers, maybe—but they have the spiritual buoyancy of a belief in

> something. That sort of belief I see in Ireland is a belief emanating from life, from nature, from revealed religion, and from the nation. A sort of dream that produces a sense of magic. Reading through the anthologies made from contemporary English poets I would say that there is little sign of such magic; indeed there are few signs of the awful sense of respect for words which poetry demands. . . . I am afraid, Mr. MacNeice, you, as an Irishman, cannot escape from your blood, nor from our blood-music that brings the racial character to mind. Irish poetry remains a creation happily, fundamentally rooted in rural civilization, yet aware of and in touch with the elementals of the future. . . .
>
> *MacNeice*: I have the feeling that you have sidetracked me into an Ireland versus England match. I am so little used to thinking of poetry in terms of race-consciousness that no doubt this was very good for me. However, I am still unconverted. I think one may have such a thing as one's racial blood-music, but that, like one's unconscious, it may be left to take care of itself. Compared with you, I take a rather common-sense view of poetry. I think that the poet is a sensitive instrument designed to record anything which interests his mind or affects his emotions. If a gasometer, for instance, affects his emotions, or if the Marxian dialectic, let us say, interests his mind, then let them come into his poetry. He will be fulfilling his function as a poet if he records these things with integrity and with as much music as he can compass or as is appropriate to the subject.

We can see how the attitudes here espoused by MacNeice are bound to be more sympathetic to Muldoon, who is also a writer of the ironical and distancing sort; and we are also painfully aware at this fifty-year distance how Higgins's innocent burble about blood-music has become malignant in retrospect, tainted with the stain of Nazi ideology and Aryan racism. So the whole introduction would seem to represent a settled case, a neatly adjudicated verdict which vindicates the case of the prosecution against hazy romantic notions about th the poet's bardic relation to territory and inheritance; a verdict favouring the sceptical over the committed, the cosmopolitan over the national, the lightness of detachment over the heaviness of attachment. Moreover, Muldoon's positioning of this extract at the front of a book of Irish poetry, which incidentally includes a generous selection of MacNeice's work, would seem also to declare the fatuousness of any further discussion of the question which Derek Mahon avers can clear a room faster than any other: Is Louis MacNeice an English or an Irish poet?

One agrees with Muldoon's implied impatience. MacNeice is clearly an Irish poet who positioned his lever in England and from that position moved his Irish subject matter through a certain revealing distance. The provinciality of his feeling, that attribute which Thomas Hardy believed to be contributory to good poetry, was an English provinciality. To include him in an anthology of Irish poetry is to affirm in a politically useful way that the category of Irishness is no longer confined to persons with the native blood-thrum but has been expanded to include people of Irish birth who wish to be allowed the rights to all the other dimensions integral to their memory and their heritage.

Yet however neatly we want this verdict to be handed down, however elegantly we may wish to quarantine the sophistications and double-understandings of the poetic sophistications and double-understandings of the poetic imagination from the solidarities and antagonism of politics, these latter troublesome complexities keep nagging at MacNeice and Muldoon also, in an imaginatively rewarding way. MacNeice puts it like this in his English-based meditation, "Suite for Recorders":

> Pride in your history is pride
> In living what your fathers died,
> Is pride in taking your own pulse
> And counting in you someone else.
> . . .
>
> Your Alter Egos, present, past,
> Or future even, could not last
> Did your word only prove them true;
> Though you choose them, yet they chose you.

This is much more laid-back than Higgins, but in fact reinforces some of Higgins's claims. Taking a pulse and counting it is the idiom we might expect from a man who thinks of the poet as a sensitive instrument; it sounds scientific, but it still is acknowledging the relevance of concerns which are embarrassing when formulated in terms of "race-consciousness" or "racial blood-music."

MacNeice, in other words, is honest but cautious in the area where the act of poetry begins to have meaning in the light of history and politics, and while part of this caution derives from the European scene in the 1930's, part of it is also derived from MacNeice's original sense of complication and ambivalence as a consciousness with a Western Irish dream life and a West British intellectual life. Auden had declared in his Introduction to *The Poet's Tongue* (1935) that "Poetry is not concerned with telling people what to do, but with extending our knowledge of good and evil, perhaps making the necessity for action more urgent and its nature more clear"; but MacNeice, with a clergyman father who had once preached a sermon in favour of Home Rule for Ireland to a congregation of Northern Irish Unionists, had more than a theoretical understanding of the difference between extending people's knowledge of good and evil and telling them what to do. Willy nilly, he was involved in Irish experience, north and south, by reason of birth and ancestry; so involved, in fact, as to have a second division in himself ancillary to the overarching Ireland/England one. This was the tension between the civil Anglo-Ireland of Nationalist sympathy and Connemara scenery from which his father sprang, the Ireland of Lady Gregory and Douglas Hyde and John M. Synge, and another Ireland, a Calvinist, abrasive and increasingly militant Ulster of Orange bands and stern-faced Unionist magnates, facing down the voluble resentments of the Catholic ghettoes.

In many respects, MacNeice's pre-natal mountain resembled Yeats's Ben Bulben. It stood in a western landscape which was his father's native ground and it shimmered with an aura of pastoral; it remembered an Ireland previous to the fall into urban sectarianism and political faction, and it retained a visionary appeal for him in spite of his accustomed guardedness and irony—for MacNeice knew well how quickly the gleam in a romantic poet's eye could convert to the glint in the eye of a sniper. In "Carrick Revisited," the whole parallelogram of cultural and ancestral forces operating in MacNeice's life is discovered and thereby to a certain extent redressed. What the poem calls "the pre-natal mountain"—the locus of his vision and desire, where the blissful subsumes the infantile—is an imaginary place held in equilibrium with two other places. First, the England of his schooling and domicile, the England of adult experience, of war and work. But second, and more important in its otherness from the dream-mountain, is the plumb, assured, unshakable fact of an Ulster childhood which cannot be shed, since its intimacies and particularities are indelibly present to the consciousness that would opt beyond them—and indeed *has* opted for southern England. The poem is wonderfully honest, not superior to the downbeat of Ulster, not overly susceptible to the aura of the west of Ireland, not denying a fidelity to the chosen ground of England:

> Back to Carrick, the castle as plumb assured
> As thirty years ago—Which war was which?
> Here are new villas, here is a sizzling grid
> But the green banks are as rich and the lough as hazily lazy
> And the child's astonishment not yet cured.
>
> Who was—and am—dumbfounded to find myself
> In a topographical frame—here, not there—
> The channels of my dreams determined largely
> By random chemistry of soil and air;
> Memories I had shelved peer at me from the shelf.
>
> Fog-horn, mill-horn, corncrake and church bell
> Half-heard through boarded time as a child in bed
> Glimpses a brangle of talk from the floor below
> But cannot catch the words. Our past we know
> But not its meaning—whether it meant well.
>
> Time and place—our bridgeheads into reality
> But also its concealment! Out of the sea
> We land on the Particular and lose
> All other possible bird's-eye views, the Truth
> That is of Itself for Itself—but not for me.
>
> Torn before birth from where my fathers dwelt,
> Schooled from the age of ten to a foreign voice,
> Yet neither western Ireland nor southern England
> Cancels this interlude; what chance misspelt
> May never now be righted by my choice.

Whatever then my inherited or acquired
Affinities, such remains my childhood's frame
Like a belated rock in the red Antrim clay
That cannot at this era change its pitch or name—
And the pre-natal mountain is far away.

This poem does not purport to tell us how to act in the poll-booths in Northern Ireland. It is not a great rallying call such as sects and cults are founded upon, but it is nonetheless a clarification, a momentary stay against confusion. The move from delight to wisdom, from surprise at the initial bright shoots of childhood recognition to a composure won by recollection of all the defamiliarizations and displacements that have occurred in the meantime—this move performs the work of art. MacNeice's disaffection from Ulster does not preclude an ongoing affection, and in his resolution of this doubleness he became and remains a vital figure in the history of modern Irish poetry, one whom the poets Michael Longley, Derek Mahon and Paul Muldoon have each saluted at different times as a helpful example.

By acknowledging the drag back into the demeaning actualities of Ulster, MacNeice's poetry remains more problematically burdened than his rather brisk critical pronouncements would suggest; it is certainly not partisan, not what we would dare call "Unionist poetry" or "Nationalist poetry," yet it engages the "particular historic complex" upon which these caricatured poetic divisions are predicated. Its importance for the three poets I mention is subtly different in each case, yet overall it could be stated thus: MacNeice provides an example of how distance, either of the actual, exilic, cross-channel variety or the imaginary, self-renewing, trans-historical and trans-cultural sort, can be used as an enabling factor in the work of art in Ulster. For with MacNeice, Mahon, Longley and—above all—Muldoon, we can begin to consider how important the length of the arm of the lever is when it comes to the actual business of moving a world. This takes us back to another basic school-book principle of science, the principle of moments, the principle in operation when the claw hammer draws out the nail or the crow-bar dislodges the boulder. In each case, what is intractable when wrestled with at close quarters becomes tractable when addressed from a distance. The longer the lever, in fact, the less force is necessary to move the mass and get the work going.

We might speculate that MacNeice indeed initiates a counter-Yeatsian move in Irish poetry. Yeats declared to Sturge Moore, in relation to Thoor Ballylee, that all his art theories came down to this one, "rooting of mythology in the earth." This is the founder's need, and until the poem of the place is achieved, the imagination will be needy for it. And yet in its thankless and perverse way, the imagination will begin to uproot the mythology once it senses that it is too securely lodged. This is true, as we have seen, even within the action of Yeats's own poetry, where the compulsion to erect an historical cultural monument is matched by countervailing prayers for transcendence. If at one moment W. B. Yeats's own ancient glittering eyes can exult in the spectacle of the Dublin Municipal Gallery full of portraits of his friends in whose lineaments the future will trace the history of Ireland—an Ireland invented, as Oscar Wilde said Japan was invented, by her artists—at another moment, the ancient glittering eyes of his visionary Chinese sages can contemplate with equally intense satisfaction the obliteration of what history had settled and Yeats can join in refrain with the Great Lord Chou: Let all things pass away.

But this is to move forward into the concerns of my next lecture. I merely wish to suggest here that if one perceptible function of poetry is to write place into existence, another of its functions is to unwrite it; and a poet who, like MacNeice, diagnoses his own belatedness as a boulder far from the mountain, a vestigial stone in a world of clay, is unlikely to set about the enterprise of building up since his poetical body-clock is all set, as it were, to run down. So it may well be that MacNeice's hallucinatory last poems, set in a London where the black taxi becomes a death coach peopled with ghosts, where the bus is dreamily transformed into a Dantesque soul-mobile and the Thames boatman becomes Charon—in late poems like these and in classic early poems of the Thirties like "Bagpipe Music" and "The Sunlight on the Garden" and "Meeting Point"—it may well be we are witnessing the variously resourceful expressions of a single condition of displacement and unrest. His celebrated thematic obsession with flux, in other words, may be a consequence of his unsettled and unsettleable placing between a pre-natal Ireland, a native Ulster and an embraced England.

However that may be, there is clearly a demonstrable continuity between this poet with an imagination which conceives itself "a belated rock in the red Antrim clay" and a poet like Derek Mahon who writes the following short poem called, with an intent that could equally be described as visionary or ironical, "Nostalgias." This poem, let it be said, is the work of another poet sprung from the Protestant community in Northern Ireland, although Derek Mahon would be as grateful for being described as a Northern Protestant as James Joyce would have been for being called a Southern Catholic. Mahon is, in fact, the Stephen Dedalus of Belfast.

Nostalgias

The chair squeaks in a high wind,
Rain falls from its branches,
The kettle yearns for the
Mountain, the soap for the sea.
In a tiny stone church
On the desolate headland
A lost tribe is singing 'Abide With Me'.

The principle of moments is at work here in such a fine-drawn way that its operation may not be immediately evident to those unaccustomed to the minute inspections and pressures habitual to Ulster readers. The chair is the end-product of a tree which once lived in the forest; this timber that is nostalgic for the sway and benison of its older greenwood life is actually on the way to splitting up and breaking down into faggots and splinters. Similarly, the kettle longs for the pre-natal mountain, where the ore was mined that eventually was fashioned into its ever more and more fatigued metal. And the lost tribe on its headland singing its nostalgia for God? Needless to say, the trope can be tied down to reflect the precise historical predicament of the Northern Protestant community, its sense of election more definitively affirmed even as its sense of security is more unignorably assailed. The touch here is exhilaratingly light, but the mass moved is heavy, is indeed at a far, deep level of sympathy, "Heart smitten with emotion."

Mahon, like MacNeice, like Longley, cannot totally identify with the pieties and refusals of the group they were all three born into, those Northern Unionists bonded by heritage into political solidarity, unconceding custodians of civic power and unyielding refusers of an Irish dimension to their lives. These poets, who share an origin in the Northern Unionist majority, are in natural communion with that Irish culture of which the Unionist ideology is chronically if understandably suspicious. As poets, they comprehend both the solidarities of their own group and the need to subvert them. They could not possibly devote themselves to a project of writing a political Ulster into being on the terms which the dominant Unionist ideology would prescribe, since the only possible imaginative equivalent of the Unionist slogans "Not an Inch" and "No Surrender" would be a rigor and imperviousness of which they are incapable.

Hence, their vision of the predicament of their own spirit, which is often an analogue for and an exfoliation out of the balked predicament of their group, is typically couched in terms of release or absolution. In Mahon's poems, we have a constant recourse to the resolved stillness of painting or to timeless receptive moments of epiphany. We dwell intently upon an image from Beckett of the light gleaming a moment, or upon an image from Bashō of the snow party on the veranda at Nagoya; or we have a typical concentration on a moment of break-through, as when the last fire-king (in a variation upon J. G. Fraser's account of his fate) breaks the barbarous cycle and dies by his own hand rather than obey tradition and wait to be killed by his usurper. The most striking example of this focus upon the moment of release comes in the wonderful climax of Mahon's epoch-making poem "A Disused Shed in Co. Wexford." Here he makes the door of a shed open so that an apocalypse of sunlight blazes onto an overlooked, unpleasant yet pathetic colony of mushrooms. What they cry out, I am bold to interpret, is the querulous chorus that Mahon hears from the pre-natal throats of his Belfast ancestors, pleading from the prison of their sectarian days with the free man who is their poet-descendant:

> They are begging us, you see, in their wordless way,
> To do something, to speak on their behalf
> Or at least not to close the door again.
> Lost people of Treblinka and Pompeii
> 'Save us, save us,' they seem to say,
> 'Let the god not abandon us

Who have come so far in darkness and in pain.
We too had our lives to live.
You with your light meter and relaxed itinerary,
Let not our naive labours have been in vain!'

Earlier, I noted a scepticism about Higgins's requirement that a poem be somehow responsive to "the nation" to which the poet belongs; and I noted also a resistance to the Yeatsian demand that Irish poets cast their minds on other days in order to maintain a continuum of identity. I now would like to suggest that these commitments, discredited for the reasons I outlined, may not so much have disappeared from poetry as refined their means. Instead of tribal celebration we have a lyric irony; instead of earthy certitudes, we have visionary metamorphoses. Consider, for example, the immense distance from which Michael Longley contemplates a roadside atrocity of the early 1970s, when a small busload of Protestant linen workers were stopped on their way home from work one winter evening and shot by the IRA. The conventional expectation would be for a poem of lament and recrimination, encompassing perhaps the Protestant community's sense of outrage at the massacre. What Longley actually wrote is stunningly original and unpredictable:

Christ's teeth ascended with him into heaven:
Through a cavity in one of his molars
The wind whistles: he is fastened for ever
By his exposed canines to a wintry sky.

I am blinded by the blaze of that smile
And by the memory of my father's false teeth
Brimming in their tumbler: they wore bubbles
And, outside of his body, a deadly grin.

When they massacred the ten linen workers
There fell on the road beside them spectacles,
Wallets, small change, and a set of dentures:
Blood, food particles, the bread, the wine.

Before I can bury my father once again
I must polish the spectacles, balance them

> Upon his nose, fill his pockets with money
> And into his dead mouth slip the set of teeth.

The poem begins with a proposition that promises a surreal comedy—Christ's teeth ascending with him into heaven—but it actually delivers a horrendous melodrama. The crucifixion is reimagined for what it must have been, a howling animal death, open-jawed against the sky; the technical enumeration of canines and molars savagely rubs our readers' noses in the physicality and extremity of Christ's cry, and banishes all the stock-response consolation there might be in linking the redemptive death of the victim on the cross with the death of the roadside victims in Co. Armagh.

But then the poem swerves once more, to hit a panicky note of zany Daliesque hallucination. What are Longley's father's dentures doing here? For here they indisputably are, articulated, effervescent, brilliantly alone and grinning. They are here because they spring up, unbidden and uncanny, once the poet learns that in the convulsions of the shot workers by the roadside, a set of false teeth, bloodied and stained with food particles, fell to the ground. They are here to be replaced in his dead father's mouth as an act of sympathetic magic. The banal marvel of bodily wholeness restored through the fitting of a set of dentures is a sacramental rite to signify the desired world-miracle of wrongs redressed and wholeness restored through the intervention of the act of poetry itself.

Yet I wonder if there is not another step to be taken in the explication of "The Linen Workers"? Within the corpus of Longley's work, his father appears as in life he actually was, the Englishman in Ulster, the ex-British soldier branded forever by his experiences on the Western Front, dying in the end from a cancer that woke in his old war wounds. So in this most far-fetched and intimately daring elegy, is it pressing things too far to presume, in the words of David Jones, that "what is evoked, invoked or incanted, is in some way or another . . . essentially bound up with the particular historic complex" to which the dead belong? The particular complex in this case is one which encompasses the inner system of attachments, affections and predispositions shared by the workers as Protestant Ulstermen; by Longley's father, as British soldier and witness of the Ulster Division's demented courage at the Somme;

and by the word "linen" itself as emblematic of the Ulster Planter myth of industry, dissent and self-reliance.

I propose this reading to further MacNeice's insight that "Alter Egos, present, past,/Or future even, could not last/Did your word only prove them true;/Though you choose them, yet they chose you"; and to prove that when he says to Higgins that one's unconscious can be left to look after itself, he was actually, whether he liked it or not, speaking a truth beyond the common-sense that he professed. We might say that those poets who consciously refuse to punt along on the currents of communal feeling are rewarded by the Muse with an onset of subliminal energy and a truly poetic expression of the common plight.

She has certainly been generous on this score to Paul Muldoon, whom I quoted earlier in the lecture, and whose swerves away from any form of poker-faced solidarity with the political programs of the Northern Catholic minority (from which he hails) have kept him so much on his poetic toes that he has practically achieved the poetic equivalent of walking on air. From the very beginning—when the stealthy indigenous ways of North American Indians were his mask for the native resource of his own enterprise, or when the activity of a military field hospital during the American Civil War was an allegory for the correct activity of poets in the divided parishes of Northern Ireland—down to his latest poems where a cast of British and European artists assemble in Brooklyn to free-associate on the theme of art and life, this poet has had an exquisite, fantastical, even virtuoso understanding of the principle of moments in poetry. His lever for the Troubles has never been less than the proverbial forty-foot pole, and yet paradoxically he has managed to relay the vehemence and squalor and helplessly self-validating energies which have characterized the history of the last twenty years. He absconded, like Auden, from a native audience's expectation that he would play "the war poet" and act as a kind of home guard on the domestic front. Yet in his completely artistic compulsion to use the deposits of early Irish legend and literature—in his brilliant redeployment of the *immram* motif, for example, which is a specifically Celtic aspect of the quest theme—Muldoon has also verified by symbolic invention the kind of gallivanting statement he must have winced at even as he included it in his prologue. "The sort of belief I see in Ireland," Higgins declared there, "is a belief emanating from life . . . A sort of dream that produces a sense of magic." The final irony, for which we must all be grateful, is that it was the ironist himself who produced the goods capable of transfusing new life into that apparently doomed and simple vision.

Cornucopia and Empty Shell: Variations on a Theme from Ellmann

Later in the lecture I will address directly the theme from Ellmann. I begin with a variation I played on it a few years ago when I wrote a poem called "The Disappearing Island." The voice that speaks in it is informed by a memory of what transpired when St. Brendan the Navigator landed with his monks on a barren but nonetheless welcome island in the western ocean. For them, it was a place of refuge, a locus of penitential discipline and potentially a home where they might settle for good. Yet after their first night of respite on its shores, the island turned over, revealed itself as a wakened sea-monster and promptly disappeared into the waves:

> Once we presumed to found ourselves for good
> Between its blue hills and those sandless shores
> Where we spent our desperate night in prayer and vigil,
>
> Once we had gathered driftwood, made a hearth
> And hung our cauldron like a firmament,
> The island broke beneath us like a wave.
>
> The land sustaining us seemed to hold firm
> Only when we embraced it *in extremis*.
> All I believe that happened there was vision.

The double-take of that last line is what I am concerned with in this third lecture on the place of writing: the speaker who had the experience of his island does not know what value he is to assign to it and treads the tightrope of his uncertainty in a line that stretches between two opposing truths. First, everything that seemed to happen there was hallucination, unreliably subjective, self-deluding even, and therefore not to be credited; and second, precisely because the experience was self-born and possessed the eerie lucidity of dream-vision, its unique aura transcends the banal reliabilities of the usual and commands the assent of awakened imagination. This latter disposition—to privilege the oneiric over the actual—finds its extreme expression in Oscar Wilde's declaration that "nothing that actually occurs is of the slightest importance," while the former finds its champion in Dr. Samuel Johnson, who famously confounded Bishop Berkeley's idealism by kicking a stone, thereby committing himself to what Yeats called the preposterous, pragmatical pigginess of the world.

The place of writing, as Yeats envisaged it and as the biographer of St. Brendan the Navigator practiced it, was to overbear this "pig of a world," and so write place into imaginative reality. Indeed Joyce's purpose to forge the uncreated conscience of his race could be read as part of the same impulse. Joyce moved like a great factory ship, unlooked for and inexorable, hoovering up every form of life on the seafloor of the Irish psyche, from the most evasive and scuttling dishonesties to the most hampered and crustacean petrifactions. In his exhaustiveness lies his exhilaration. By dividing the torpid consciousness of his race against itself, by giving it an affronting image of itself, he still fortified it even as he castigated it, and thereby justified the potentially overbearing claim he made to Grant Richards in 1906 that his literary purpose consisted in "the spiritual liberation of my country."

Yet obviously, in the case of both Yeats and Joyce, what the poet Patrick Kavanagh would later call "the messianic impulse," the drive to inflame people with a livable truth, was secondary to the artistic impulse itself. This impulse which I defined earlier and perhaps too briefly as the need to raise historical circumstance to a symbolic power, the need to move personal force through an aesthetic distance, this impulse both fulfills and exhausts itself at the limit of the artist's powers in the achievement of art work. After this extreme moment, the poetry enters into another press of carryover, when it is "modified in the guts of the living." This is the process by which Yeats and Joyce, again in Auden's words, "became [their] admirers"; by which (in terms of a newer idiom) their texts became canonical. At that point—and the responses of Patrick Kavanagh and Paul Muldoon to the achievement of Yeats are an example of this—a dialectic is set in motion in which the new writing does not so much displace the old as strive to displace itself to an enabling distance away from it.

This perception—that any writing is to some extent an unwriting not only of previous writings but even of itself—is one that has been greatly elaborated into systems of reading. Yet it is more the critical procedure deriving from it than the perception itself which is new. Indeed my theme from Ellmann concerns this doubleness of the fully empowered imagination, its compulsion to unwind the winding path, to encompass within its lift-off an acknowledgement of the gravity that pulls it down. In his lecture on "W. B. Yeats's Second Puberty" Richard Ellmann, writing with great clarity and finality, lays out the Yeatsian aspect of this truth as follows:

> He could conceive of nothing as empty and also as pregnant. . . . As Yeats reached his life's end, he recognized that he would never be able to decide between the beatific vision and its obverse. The image of life as cornucopia was relentlessly undermined by the image of life as an empty shell. . . . The artist imposes form upon the void but knows that the void may yet overwhelm. In the fiery furnaces where universes are made they may yet go to die. "The painter's brush consumes his dreams," Yeats wrote, and knew that the poet's pen belongs similarly to a process of decreation as much as of creation.

It is the disconsolateness of this helplessly recurring awareness that makes for the greatness and modernity of Yeats's work. Over his whole career, and within particular works such as *At the Hawk's Well* and "The Circus Animals' Desertion" (to both of which I shall return), we see artistic creation not simply as a habit of verse-making and a pursuit of a national cultural ambition but as a way of knowledge challenging the poet to live by the truths it discloses. The turbulent self-questioning of a late poem like "Man and the Echo" in which, in Ellmann's words, Yeats "was obliged by his inner honesty to allow for the possibility that reality was desolation and justice a figment," this existential, heuristic ferocity is at once continuous with and recoils upon the passionately earthed certitude of earlier pieces like "Red Hanrahan's Song About Ireland" or *Cathleen Ni Houlihan* or even "Easter, 1916." At the end, the founder stands dumbfounded:

> What do we know but that we face

One another in this place?

These are the last-ditch words of the man, instructed in hopelessness by the echo's portentous "Lie down and die," "Into the night." Yeats has committed himself to "The spiritual intellect's great work," the arrangement of reality "In one clear view," yet such a game of knowledge can only end in stalemate. Nevertheless, it is the embrace of this stalemate, the capacity to brave it out as the island disappears and the wood moves, that distinguishes such mature and indispensible works as those I now wish to address.

If Paul Muldoon has rewritten the Yeatsian *immram* and punished the longing and complaint of *The Wanderings of Oisin* with his prodigiously knowledgeable longer poems such as "Immram" itself and "The More a Man Has the More a Man Wants," it is Thomas Kinsella, his senior by some twenty-odd years, who has engaged the mature Yeats's compulsion to be in love and to love what vanishes. Since the late sixties, this deeply responsible poet has been absorbed in a slowly purposeful, heroically undeflected work of personal and national inquisition. From his early, formal and syntactically compact poems of the 1950s, when he defined his purpose as the quest for honesty in love and art, to his more recent, open-weave, semi-expressionist explorations at the roots of consciousness, the muscle tone of Kinsella's poetry has always been in perfect order. The subject of much of his work is found in the ever-present wash of acedia and inanition round the edges of a life or a purpose, yet the pitch of the work is antithetically intense and capable.

Two short poems from different periods of his career will be enough to show how Kinsella's poetry belongs with the concerns of this lecture and how his technical and imaginative processes have developed. The first is from a sequence of tightly rhymed and strictly argued epigrams, entitled *Moralities,* which appeared in 1960. The sequence has four divisions subtitled, with challenging bareness, Faith, Love, Death and Song. Half-way through, between the emblem poems on love and those on death, comes this quotation, out of series, entitled "Interlude":

Love's doubts enrich my words; I stroke them out.
To each felicity, once. He must progress

Who fabricates a path, though all about
Death, Woman, Spring, repeat their first success.

I have used the word "theme." To say "theme" too often in the discussion of modern poetry is to be reminded sooner or later of Robert Graves's grammar of poetic myth, *The White Goddess*; there Graves elaborates his conviction that there is one theme, one story and one story only, behind true poems, since they all recount some episode in the eternal struggle between the god of the waxing year and the god of the waning year for the hand of the goddess. This is another way of expressing what Yeats was seeking to give shape to in his model of reality as two interpenetrating cones or gyres, the one waning to an apex where the other waxes to a base. It is also another aspect of the cornucopia developing its image out of its negative in the empty shell. Kinsella comes through as a poet helplessly burdened with all the recognitions that these schemes hold up to the mind's eye for contemplation.

The first line of his "Interlude" keeps the ball of meaning in the air, fleetly bouncing back off the wall of one possibility to the opposite wall, to and fro across a definitely placed caesura. "Love's doubts enrich my words; I stroke them out." So does he stroke out the words or does he stroke out the doubts? If he strokes out the doubts and keeps the enriched words, there is no honesty either in the words or in the love. If he strokes out the words, there is no honest acknowledgement that love's doubts are the corollary of love's enrichments. It is a bind from which he would not be released because of an imposed discipline of understanding. The voice of that discipline is the true voice of Kinsella's muse; in the contexts of sexual and domestic love, biological and spiritual survival, physical and psychological exhaustions and renewals—all of which Kinsella takes for granted as what he calls simply "the ordeal"—this muse speaks the same command over and over again throughout Kinsella's poetry. Deeper, she says. Further. Don't repose in the first resolution of your predicament. That resolution too is a predicament. What more? "Nothing will come of nothing. Speak again." Forge on. Fabricate the path.

Love's doubts enrich my words; I stroke them out.
To each felicity, once. He must progress

Who fabricates a path, though all about
Death, Woman, Spring, repeat their first success.

The formal ancestry of "Interlude" may include the Auden of "Death of a Tyrant" and the epigrammatic side of Pope and Donne and Jonson. But the formal ancestry of the later short poem which I will read goes back to early Irish glosses, those brief rhapsodies of the scribe in the margin as he breaks free from the illumination of the great Latin of Holy Writ into the intimate vernacular of the Old Irish language. Often these verses catch a glimpse of a creature—a blackbird or a seal or a cat—or of a joyful moment in the wood. The radiance of a God-filled and divinely ordained nature is implicit in each little pleasure spurt from the hermit's pen. In Kinsella's gloss, on the other hand, a post-Darwinian nature instructs the self in the necessity for constant self-digestion as the condition of self-creation, the laws of psychic life being discernible analogically at the extremes of biological survival. This is Thomas Kinsella's "Leaf-Eater":

On a shrub in the heart of the garden,
On an outer leaf, a grub twists
Half its body, a tendril,
This way and that in blind
Space: no leaf or twig
Anywhere in reach; then gropes
Back on itself and begins
To eat its own leaf.

This little poem appeared in Kinsella's volume, *Nightwalker and Other Poems* (1968). In that book, he was negotiating his transition from an earlier poetry that was primarily informed by the musical strains of the English poetic line and operated within an English tradition of the meditative or witty poem of definite closure. *Nightwalker* moved towards a different poetry of the open, modernist, Poundian sort, responsive and ongoing, disinclined to the sedateness of traditional stanzaic articulation, content to be fluid and fragmented, yet never mistaking the randomness of this method for permission to slacken intellectual grip on the poem's purpose. The more open Kinsella's poetry becomes formally, the more insistent and integrated becomes its obsession with "the theme."

His recoil from the entropic conditions of the modern Irish scene into the nutrient original deposits of early Irish literary and legendary matter finds its analogue in the leaf-eater's solution to its predicament. "I feed upon it still, as you see," he declares in another context. In yet another, the grub's energies that waved with exploratory zeal on the edge of a leaf are repossessed by a questing, founding consciousness when "A maggot of the possible-wriggled out of the spine/into the brain."

These lines are taken from "Finistére," a poem in Kinsella's strong late manner. In it, Kinsella deliberately embarks upon the mythic method of Pound's early cantos, where psychic and literary faring forth is commingled with the venturings of Homeric and Ovidian heroes. In Kinsella's case, the mythic history of Ireland, as told in the early part of *The Book of Invasions,* provides the wave on which his individual poetic voice can row along. In particular, Kinsella fixes on the arrival in Ireland of the sons of Mil, the supplanters not only of the Formorian denizens but also of the Tuatha de Danaan. Along with Mil and his people there arrives, as the voice of their collective wisdom and purpose, the bard Amergin, ur-poet of the island of Ireland. Through the reappropriation of Amergin's old lines, Kinsella once again rehearses the motif of renewal at the point of exhaustion: the tremor of development arrives involuntarily out of the detritus of a previous life: "A maggot of the possible/wriggled out of the spine/into the brain." This is an image of the stirred power experienced by Amergin when he set foot on the land and spoke the prophetic lines which Kinsella appropriates in order to transmit a feeling of his own empowerment. This new capacity for accommodating (within the ordering principle of the archetype) both the data of the contemporary and the poet's own autobiographical projects has vastly extended Kinsella's poetic scope and accrued a body of work that marks an important stage in the evolution not just of Irish poetry but of modern poetry in English.

The peculiar modernity of it has much to do with the enforcement of a recognition which Ellmann pointed to in Yeats—that nothingness could be pregnant as well as empty. This recognition is orchestrated fully in a strange poem called "Hen Woman," the anecdotal base of which is quickly stated. In a country farmyard, on a still, sunlit afternoon, a child watches with eye-popping, almost erotic fascination as an egg begins to be laid by a hen. The thing is played in slow motion; the egg appears in the sphincter, the woman of the house rushes to catch it, misses, the egg falls and breaks on an iron grating, spills down into the sewage, is wasted, gone, lost, like seed that falls on barren ground, like spilled potential, obliterated possibility, whatever. Yet just as the fall of a sparrow is to the heavenly father a matter of infinite concern, to be cherished throughout all eternity, so the fall of an egg places absolute demands upon poetic imagination and tests its ability to plump the shell with its own ghostly plenitude:

> I feed upon it still, as you see;
> there is no end to that which,
> not understood, may yet be noted
> and hoarded in the imagination,
> in the yolk of one's being, so to speak,
> there to undergo its (quite animal) growth,
> dividing blindly,
> twitching, packed with will,
> searching in its own tissue
> for the structure
> in which it may wake.
> Something that had—clenched
> in its cave—not been
> now was: an egg of being.
> Through what seemed a whole year it fell
> —as it still falls, for me,
> solid and light, the red gold beating
> in its silvery womb,
> alive as the yolk and white
> of my eye; as it will continue
> to fall, probably, until I die,
> through the vast indifferent spaces
> with which I am empty.

"I only know things seem and are not good," says Kinsella, in the first line of "Nightwalker." And in the last, "I think this is the Sea of Disappointment." And he once confessed, in relation to his annual moves between a home in Dublin and a professorship at Temple University in Philadelphia, that while he found it more and more necessary to return to Ireland, he also found it less and less rewarding. All this is of a piece with the extremity and exactions that characterize his poetic achievement. Indeed, when Yeats declared "Those men that in their writings are most wise/Own nothing but their blind, stupefied hearts," he was giving us a way of reading Kinsella, a poet who has discovered a completely satisfactory form for his dissatisfactions and sense of incompleteness.

This is not the place to explicate the coherence of Kinsella's *oeuvre.* Suffice it to say that he has ingested loss—of a literature in the Irish language, of a political vision in post-Independence Ireland, of all that time robs from the original resources of the individual psyche—and has remembered it in an art that has the effect of restitution. The place of waste, the place of renewal and the place of writing have become co-terminous within the domain of his poetry—and nowhere more luminously than in the concluding lines of "His Father's Hands." This poem recounts, among other things, how the child poet used to hammer into a wooden block little nails which his cobbler-grandfather used for shoe repairs; in the end, even these unregarded trivia are made to swarm with larval possibility, retrieved by memory and hatched into a second life by the intent imagination:

> Extraordinary . . . The big block—I found it
> years afterward in a corner of the yard
> in sunlight after rain
> and stood it up, wet and black:
> it turned under my hands, an axis
> of light flashing down its length,
> and the wood's soft flesh broke open,
> countless little nails
> squirming and dropping out of it.

This delicacy and vigor of notation is essential to Kinsella's poetry, as is the amplification of suggestion that occurs when we connect those squirming nails with "a maggot of the possible," and a grub that twists and gropes back on itself. Each poetic occasion in this oeuvre is situated within a deliberated perspective. One is aware of a strong objective intellect and an indignant sensibility cleaving to a purpose that is intensely personal and yet is proffered as a standard and a reminder. Kinsella is, in fact, the representative Irish poet in that his career manifests the oath-bound, unrewarded plight of the *comitatus* in Yeats's black tower. In his work, we can watch the ancient correspondence between the nation's possibilities and the imagination of its poet—represented originally by the Milesian bard Amergin—discover itself again in a modern drama of self-knowledge and self-testing.

That drama and correspondence are recurrent features of the writer's vocation in Ireland. A feeling of being oath-bound and a recognition of the possible vacuousness of the binding force, these things haunt any Irish writer who "evokes, invokes or incants" imaginative stuff bound up with the particular historic complex that Thomas Flanagan once designated "the matter of Ireland." I have looked at the way the banished ghost of this matter reappears to haunt the exorcist, be he a Muldoon or a MacNeice, and the way it remains importunate as an incubus upon writers like Yeats or Kinsella who raised it by their original concitations. In the remaining part of this lecture, I want briefly to trace the pattern home in works by Irish playwrights; and I shall then conclude by reading a poem of John Montague's as a coda to the overall survey I have been conducting.

In Brian Friel's play, *Faith Healer* (1980), we have a representation of the disappointed return to Ireland of a dilapidated Irish faith healer who has spent a life on the road in Britain, swayed between intimations of himself as a charlatan and fleeting convictions about the marvel of his gift. The parallel with the Irish writer's problematical relation to his given ground is obvious, and the climax of Friel's play is devastating. Frank Hardy has come back, has attended a boozy wedding, has got involved with the menace of the local young bloods in their drink, and has inevitably been drawn into the challenge to heal their disabled friend, a dumbly hurting figure called McGarvey. In Frank Hardy's recollection of what happened next, Friel's play achieves its heartbreaking conclusion:

> I poured a drink for myself. A small Irish with an equal amount of water. The thought occurred to me to get drunk but I dismissed it as . . . inappropriate. Then I heard the car return and stop outside. A silence. Then Donal's head round the door.
>
> 'McGarvey's here. But he's shy about coming in. Come you

out. They're waiting for you out there in the yard.'

'Coming,' I said. . . .

I would like to describe that yard to you.

It was a September morning, just after dawn. The sky was orange and everything glowed with a soft radiance—as if each detail of the scene had its own self-awareness and was satisfied with itself.

The yard was a perfect square enclosed by the back of the building and three high walls. And the wall facing me as I walked out was breached by an arched entrance.

Almost in the centre of the square but a little to my left was a tractor and a trailer. In the back of the trailer were four implements: there was an axe and there was a crowbar and there was a mallet and there was a hayfork. They were resting against the side of the trailer.

In the corners facing me and within the walls were two mature birch trees and the wind was sufficient to move them.

The ground was cobbled but pleasant to walk on because the cobbles were smooth with use.

And I walked across that yard, over those worn cobbles, towards the arched entrance, because framed in it, you would think posed symmetrically, were the four wedding guests; and in front of them, in his wheelchair, McGarvey. . . . A figure of infinite patience, of profound resignation, you would imagine. Not a hint of savagery. And Ned's left hand protectively on his shoulder.

And although I knew that nothing was going to happen, nothing at all, I walked across the yard towards them. And as I walked I became possessed of a strange and trembling intimation: that the whole corporeal world—the cobbles, the trees, the sky, whose four malign implements—somehow they had shed their physical reality and had become mere imaginings, and that in all existence there was only myself and the wedding guests. And that intimation in turn gave way to a stronger sense: that even we had ceased to be physical and existed only in spirit, only in the need we had for each other.

[*He takes off his hat as if he were entering a church and holds it at his chest. He is both awed and elated. As he speaks the remaining lines he moves very slowly down stage.*]

And as I moved across that yard toward them and offered myself to them, then for the first time I had a simple and genuine sense of home-coming. Then for the first time there was no atrophying terror; and the maddening questions were silent.

At long last I was renouncing chance.
[*Pause for about four seconds. Then quick black.*]

These curtain lines of Brian Friel's *Faith Healer* are like a reprise of much that I have been concerned with. In the large simple scheme of the narrative, Frank Hardy, the Irish faith healer, is returning home to his original place. The reward for this commitment is a blank and hostile stare, the malignity of those he would embrace concentrated back upon him as the antithesis of the benignity he would exercise upon them. This is like the moment when Yeats, having committed his individual talent to an idea of tradition and community, burns off those lovely entrancing scales from his eyes and commits himself instead to "a man who does not exist." In his poem "The Fisherman," when Yeats has "looked in the face/What [he] had hoped 'twould be/To write for [his] own race/And the reality," he is suffering what Frank Hardy, in a much more drastic way, has come home to. For Hardy is also being forced to look into that space which opens between hope and reality, into an effulgence that most of us prefer to close our eyes to, the light of imagination which invites us to sacrifice our actual situation to a vision of our possibilities which is doomed to fail.

Frank Hardy, the faith healer, is actually creating conditions where he is bound to fail in an exemplary way—as an example to himself. He manifests tragically the revelation vouchsafed in a comic yet macabre story about the last man to be hanged in Crumlin Road Jail in Belfast. It is said that just before this simple and chastened murderer was led to the scaffold, he turned to the priest who had been his confessor during those last hours and said, in words at once ingratiating, self-critical and hilarious, "Father, this is going to be a lesson to me."

Frank Hardy walks as certainly towards what he calls "the implements" and towards his ghastly shadow-self in the paralysed figure of McGarvey as the Crumlin Road malefactor walked towards the rope. He also proceeds with the same mixture of self-castigation and self-affirmation. When he says he is "renouncing chance" he means that the fulfillments that came involuntarily as the result of the unpredictable but departed efficacy of his faith-healing gift are no longer to be either hoped for or credited. Here Frank's creator, the artist Brian Friel, is expressing in terms of the faith-healing parable *his* awareness for the necessity in the mature artist of a preparedness for a *via negativa.* As dramatist, in other words, Friel is working in a line that goes back through Beckett's *Krapp's Last Tape* (1959) to Yeats's *At the Hawk's Well* (1917), two plays which, like *Faith Healer,* hold up to the ear of mature experience the cornucopia of young trust in the possibilities of love and transcendence, and hear only their attenuated playback in the empty shell. In these works there is no attempt to hide the fact of disappointment; an unabated desire for more beats at a shut gate above which is discovered the legend, "You must settle for less."

In the penultimate speech of the Beckett play, Krapp, the old man who is reliving with apparent scorn an earlier life preserved on his tapes, is given these lines:

> Just been listening to that stupid bastard I took myself for thirty years ago, hard to believe I was ever as bad as that. Thank God that's all done with anyway. (*Pause.*) The eyes she had! (*Broods, realizes he is recording silence, switches off, broods. . . .*)

The vision of the young man is not recorded on the tapes we hear during the action, but the young Krapp's approach to what he does indeed call "the vision" has been intimated on one tape—Box 3, Spool 5—which also includes his abounding memory of sexual fullness. The play's final speech belongs again to the voice of that tape, the voice of cornucopia, but it is being listened to within the acoustic of the empty shell. Here is the conclusion of the last speech we hear from the older Krapp, followed by young Krapp's voice on the tape that compels him back again and again:

> Be again on Croghan on a Sunday morning, in the haze, with the bitch, stop and listen to the bells. (*Pause.*) And so on. (*Pause.*) Be again, be again. (*Pause.*) All that old misery. (*Pause.*) Once wasn't enough for you. (*Pause.*) Lie down across her.
>
> *Long pause. He suddenly bends over machine, switches off, wrenches off tape, throws it away, puts on the other, winds it forward to the passage he wants, switches on, listens staring front.*

TAPE —gooseberries, she said. I said again I thought it was hopeless and no good going on, and she agreed, without opening her eyes. (*Pause.*) I asked her to look at me and after a few moments—(*pause*)—after a few moments she did, but the eyes just slits, because of the glare. I bent over her to get them in the shadow and they opened. (*Pause. Low.*) Let me in. (*Pause.*) We drifted in among the flags and stuck. The way they went down, sighing, before the stem! (*Pause.*) I lay down across her with my face in her breasts and my hand on her. We lay there without moving. But under us all moved, and moved us, gently up and down, and from side to side.

Pause. Krapp's lips move. No sound.

Past midnight. Never knew such silence. The earth might be uninhabited.

Pause.

Here I end this reel. Box—(*pause*)—three, spool—(*pause*)—five. (*Pause.*) Perhaps my best years are gone. When there was a chance of happiness. But I wouldn't want them back. Not with the fire in me now. No, I wouldn't want them back.

Krapp motionless staring before him. The tape runs on in silence.

CURTAIN

This connects not only with Yeats's play *At the Hawk's Well*, but also with his poem "The Circus Animals' Desertion"; both express a reflexiveness that hovers between amusement at the younger, more driven self, and a deep, abiding envy of him. The fire in Krapp as young self and tape-voice is invisible to us who see before us only the cold grate of his incontinent, banana-eating body; even so, we can sense in him a refreshing rage at what he has previously called "this old muckball, all the light and dark and famine and feasting." In Krapp's regenerative embrace of the negative aspect of things, he resembles the Yeats who lies down "where all the ladders start/In the foul rag and bone shop of the heart." Yet Krapp, more than Yeats ever would, has collapsed into the unspooling, run-down rhythm of his days. At his moment of similar recognition, Yeats makes positive recourse to the re-winding, spool-filling, perne-packing, time-defying act of metrical poetry—even though, as we have seen, his poetry in the last phase dances upon an acknowledgement of its own possible fatuity.

At the Hawk's Well, written more than thirty years earlier, addressed these themes also. There the paraphernalia of the Celtic Twilight—the heroic-legendary represented by Cuchulain and the folk-magical represented by a dry well which periodically brims with the water of immortality—this paraphernalia which Yeats first assembled in the cause of a national literary purpose is here worked through a second symbolic distance to become effective in rendering truth of a more universal and personally vindicating sort. We are at that thrilling moment when the place of writing shifts its locus into psychic space. The one splash of well water and the rustle of its dry leaves embody respectively a fullness of intent in the young quester in search of the immortalizing draft and the minimal but unstilled expectations of the old survivor. Here it is not a disappearing island but a non-appearing water that engages the passions of the characters, who (as avatars of the waxing and waning gods) contend for the favor of the goddess in her role as Guardian of the Well.

Here too, in a play written the year before the Easter Rebellion of 1916, we might find an allegory of Yeats's inner conflict at that moment of political crisis. In the play the young man goes off, inflamed by the entrancing hawk-eyes of the guardian of the well, while still vowing *not* to go off until he has grown immortal. The hawk-woman actually leads him away from the miraculous plash of the water; and that plash occurs when the old man falls into a doze as he covers his head and eyes from her otherworldly gaze. Her terrible beauty that rouses the young Cuchulain with the clash of arms and lures him away from the purer miracle of the well, this same beauty scares the old man into a caution that is equally a deception and an inadequate response to the demands of the governing reality. It would not be hard to imagine a reading of "Easter, 1916" in terms of *At the Hawk's Well*—Cuchulain's heart

"Enchanted to a stone," the old man murmuring "England may keep faith"—but it is a diminution of the play's chastity and strangeness to tie it down simply as a writing about its place and time. It is rather a vision in which the rising and falling of the well's waters, always occurring when we are not there, represent what Wallace Stevens called "the necessary angel" of the imagination. These occurrences also represent what T. S. Eliot called "the deception of the thrush"; and one might think too of the dry gourd in Robert Frost's poem "Directive" from which one must drink in order to be whole again beyond confusion.

The Old Man at the Hawk's Well defines himself to the Young Man as

> One whom the dancers cheat. I came like you
> When young in body and in mind, and blown
> By what had seemed to me a lucky sail.
> The well was dry, I sat upon its edge,
> I waited the miraculous flood, I waited
> While the years passed and withered me away.
> I have snared the birds for food and eaten grass
> And drunk the rain, and neither in dark nor shine
> Wandered too far away to have heard the plash,
> And yet the dancers have deceived me.

Deceive him the dancers may have done. Yet he sacrifices himself to that deception because of his conception of himself as somebody committed to a vision, exemplary in his refusal of what Ellmann called "brute fact and the standards offered by social reality." In Yeats's last poem, he seems to reappear like a shell with dew upon it, the necessary anti-self to the men of the black tower; he is watcher, bird snarer and gossipy old cook, still as full of unheeded warnings here as he was by the edge of the Hawk's Well:

> The tower's old cook that must climb and clamber
> Catching small birds in the dew of morn
> When we hale men lie stretched in slumber
> Swears that he hears the great king's horn.
> But he's a lying hound;
> Stand we on guard oath-bound!

As the imagined genius of an already imagined tower, *genus loci* of the place of writing, the old cook creates the mocking echo which is the ultimate test of fully committed vocation. And he disappears into the morning with the same mixture of scepticism and intention that characterizes the eagle in John Montague's marvelous poem of place and vision, "Mount Eagle," with which I would like to conclude.

"Mount Eagle" is about a place on the map and a state of mind, and feels like one of those gifts which sail into the ken as a poet's reward. Since definitively early poems such as "Old Mythologies" and "Like Dolmens round My Childhood, the Old People," Montague has been fated to re-enter the rough field of personal and historical memory. Since he is inclined by temperament to elegy, but compelled by circumstance to irony, the place of his writing has always been fruitfully in dispute. One part of his achievement has been a natural fulfillment of Yeats's command to keep faith with that oppressed Ireland which had been insufficiently written into English; and in *The Rough Field* (1972), as well as in many chastely rendered shorter poems, he has performed the classic lyric task of stopping time and keeping language. But another part of his poetic intelligence is impatient with this given destiny and is impelled to break with impositions of history and pieties of place; and the bonus of this impetus comes in poems like "All Legendary Obstacles" and "She Walks Alone." The modernist and the bard have been engaged in constant emulation, smiled upon by the doubly honored goddess.

Thus, at the climax of intimate place-love in *The Rough Field*, in a lyric called "The Source," when the protagonist gropes towards the original point of the water's life and music, he finds a "nothing" that is both empty and pregnant. No native, Celtic, "ancient trout of wisdom" is discovered; instead, an energy that is written, a discharge from image, syntax and enjambement, presents itself:

            nothing but that
Wavering pulse leading to
The central heart where
The spring beat, so icy-cold
I shiver now in recollection,
Hearing its brisk, tireless

Movement over the pebbles
Beneath my feet . . .

It is hard to say whether this writing belongs more to the place or to the language, and it is precisely its equilibrium that distinguishes it as poetry.

"Mount Eagle" is a poetic self-portrait by the imagination that brought forth poems such as "The Source." It freely and opulently rehearses old motifs of attachment and affection, and equally freely plays a music of detachment and subversion. It is primal insofar as it is an example of an Irish poetic genre, *dinnseanchas,* a type of poem which tells how a place got its name. It is post-modern in that it comes late to the genre. Yet it triumphs over the handicaps of self-consciousness, attains a liberated cadence and coasts into the realms of surprise. The eagle had looked at the world with a democratic relish that Yeats would have been incapable of, but with a whimsical acuity that Beckett would have approved of. Now the time has come for him to discover a way of proceeding that is his own; and in discovering it for him, John Montague has written a poem which recapitulates much of what I have been saying not only about the place of writing but about the problematic place of the writer as well. The eagle represents the poetic destiny. He must settle for the self-negating way and through this sacrifice attain a completely symbolic force:

But now he had to enter the mountain.
Why? Because a cliff had asked him?
The whole world was changing, with one
language dying, and another encroaching,
bright with buckets, cries of children.
There seemed to be no end to them,
and the region needed a guardian—
so the mountain had told him. And

A different destiny lay before him:
to be the spirit of that mountain.
Everyone would stand in awe of him.
When he was wrapped in the mist's caul
they would withdraw because of him,
peer from behind blind, or curtain.

When he lifted his wide forehead
bold with light, in the morning,
they would all laugh and smile with him.
It was a greater task than an eagle's
aloofness, but sometimes, under his oilskin
of coiled mist, he sighed for lost freedom.